SCHIRRA'S
SPACE

NASA

SCHIRRA'S SPACE

Wally Schirra
with Richard N. Billings

BLUEJACKET BOOKS

NAVAL INSTITUTE PRESS / ANNAPOLIS, MARYLAND

Originally published by Quinlan Press.
First Bluejacket Books printing, 1995

LIBRARY OF CONGRESS CATALOGING-IN-PUBLICATION DATA
Schirra, Wally.
    Schirra's space / by Walter M. Schirra, Jr. with Richard N. Billings.
        p.   cm.
    Originally published: Boston : Quinlan Press, 1988.
    ISBN 1-55750-792-9 (pbk. : alk. paper)
        1. Schirra, Wally.   2. Astronauts—United States—Biography.
I. Billings, Richard N.   II. Title.
[TL789.85.S35A3   1995]
629.45'0092—dc20
[B]   95-24817

Printed in the United States of America on acid-free paper ∞
08 07 06 05 04 03 02 01   16 15 14 13 12 11 10 9

To my wife Jo, our son Wally, and our daughter Suzanne, who helped me get out of this world three times, but who also brought me back to earth.

Contents

SCHIRRA'S
SPACE

1 Liftoff

I listened for booster engine cutoff. Two seconds early, I noted. There was a flash of light and a burst of smoke, signaling booster separation. Then the escape tower ignited, indicating tower jettison. *Sigma Seven*, my spacecraft, was now being propelled by the sustainer engine, and I hoped it would burn long enough to make me the third American to go into orbit around the earth. It worked spectacularly. I would reach an altitude of 176 miles and a speed of 17,557 miles per hour—higher and faster than any human had flown to date.

Time passed quickly as I performed the various tasks that were part of my mission. As I powered *Sigma Seven* over the Indian Ocean I switched to fly-by-wire to check the spacecraft's systems. I reported to the station in Muchea, Australia, that I sighted the moon through the window to fix my attitude and was using it as a reference point.

I knew the ground stations had been paying close attention to my fuel usage, as Mercury Control was deciding how long I'd stay up. The word came from my next-door neighbor and fellow astronaut Gus Grissom at Kauai, Hawaii: "Wally, you have a go for six orbits." "Hallelujah," I replied. A few Soviet cosmonauts had stayed in orbit for a day or more, but I was on my way to becoming the American who had flown the farthest in space.

I radioed John Glenn at Point Arguello, California, that for the next hour I'd be observing the earth and taking pictures. As I passed over Florida, I got a shot of the entire east coast, up to New England. Beautiful. I told John, "I suppose an old song, 'Drifting and Dreaming,' would be apropos at this point, but I don't have a chance to dream. I'm enjoying it too much."

What I felt during my first ride into outer space so long ago just about sums up the way I feel about my life—I've really had one hell of a good time. I've had many wonderful adventures as an astronaut, fighter pilot and test pilot. I've met some terrific people along the way, from presidents to admirals to race car drivers. And I've had the opportunity to share all this with a special friend—my wife Jo. Now this book is my opportunity to share my life and times with you.

But it's more than a chance to tell tales and remember the great friends I've met. It also gives me a chance to talk about something I feel deeply about, the space program, where we've been and where we're headed.

We were training for Apollo 7, which I commanded, when I decided to become a civilian for the first time since I was a midshipman, starting at age nineteen. I announced my decision three weeks before we launched, on October 11, 1968. I quit with mixed feelings, but I wanted to get going on the rest of my life. I'd adopted a rule of thumb about new careers. It was that they ought to begin no later than age forty five. I was due to turn forty six on March 12, 1969.

There were other reasons for retiring, and I thought about them as I recorded my thoughts in a personal debriefing right after the Apollo mission. I noted that a young engineer had remarked that I was all used up, having just flown a successful mission that got us on course toward the moon. "We cannot recycle you immediately," he said. "The space age is very hungry." I believed then and still do that the engineer was right. "It is very hungry," I said in 1968. "It devours people. I have been completely devoured by this business."

I had mulled that over for quite a while, and the wisdom of my decision seemed substantiated. "I don't feel a requirement at this point to prepare a boat for racing," I said then, "an automobile for racing, or an airplane for...high performance. From now on all vehicles for me represent a mode of transportation, not a new frontier." I've since stuck to that statement, to the point that I don't pilot a plane for

2

pleasure. Hunting and fishing and sailing are my recreations. Flying was the profession from which I retired.

I also addressed a lingering concern as I prepared for an Apollo 7 press conference at President Johnson's Texas ranch. We'd met Mr. Johnson in advance of the mission. He'd come down to the plant in Michoud, Mississippi, where they assemble the Saturn launch vehicles. "It's too bad," he said. "We have this great capability, but...we'll probably just piss it away."

My concern was along the same line. What was the objective of the space program? Had it been defined? Or was it just a one-shot effort? A stunt? "It does tend to look like a stunt," I said in 1968, "to have a crew...land on the moon and return. But I believe when we finish this particular project, we'll have proven to the world that we are capable of doing these things. Then we can focus technology, on a rather narrow path admittedly, but...man's flight in space is that, and it shall expand and continue."

I have a vivid recollection of being taken as a child to the Barnum and Bailey Circus and watching a fellow in white coveralls, the human cannonball, come roaring out of a cannon and landing in a net. I thought it was a nutty stunt, and I felt at first the same way about riding a capsule on a rocket into orbit. I considered anyone who'd do that to be out of his mind. My attitude changed eventually, but I never quite got rid of the "spam in the can" image.

We flew the can successfully, as everyone knows, and in Gemini and Apollo we got better spacecrafts, better advanced control systems—which allowed us to maneuver in space—and a computer, which enabled us to navigate a course to the moon. When Neil Armstrong and eleven other American astronauts walked on the lunar surface, we proved the space program wasn't a stunt. Or did we?

I'm not sure now. In the ultimate analysis it could have been a stunt. I don't know yet. I'm tending to lean in that direction. I do know that President Kennedy needed to emphasize a very dramatic event to offset the effect of the abortive invasion of Cuba on April 17, 1961. The first Mercury flight, Al Shepard's suborbital hop on May 5, provided an opportunity, and Kennedy grabbed it. On May 25 he announced that by the end of the decade the United States would land a man on the moon and bring him back safely. I thought it to be an unbelievable objective, since we then had not yet sent a man safely into orbit.

By 1975 our commitment to space exploration was evident. At that point, though, we veered off course. By the end of the 1980s, substantial doubts were raised about the program's purpose.

The chief culprit? The explosion of the space shuttle *Challenger,* which killed its seven-member crew. The disaster cost the U. S. its position as world leader in space exploration. And I believe it will be years before we get back on track.

I have some advice for our space planners, which I am going to sprinkle in throughout this book. I hope it's taken in the spirit it's offered—constructively. I won't pull punches, though. We are paying for a couple of basic mistakes. First, we permitted decision-making authority to be taken away from astronauts. Second, the shuttle, conceived originally to transport crew and cargo from one point to another, was turned into something else—a space laboratory and a satellite delivery system.

The solution is to return to the way it used to be. When I was one of the first seven astronauts in the early 1960's, we all were graduates of test pilot school and had earned engineering degrees to boot, enabling us to exchange ideas with the engineers . And when we felt strongly, as we often did—we were heard, about vehicle preparation, the flight plan, even policy matters. Before my Apollo mission, for example, I rejected an accelerated schedule, for it meant a seven-day work week for the technicians. I know the *Challenger* crew wasn't briefed about the condition of the O-rings on the solid rocket boosters. If it had been, the mission might have been postponed.

As for the shuttle's mission, we should again go back to the way it used to be. The logical follow-on to Apollo was and is a space station, with the shuttle supporting its development.

Shortly after the loss of *Challenger,* the space program was rocked again by the failure during liftoff of two old rockets once thought reliable: the Titan and the Delta. Those rockets were designed to put satellites into orbit. They still should be used to relieve the shuttle of its delivery mission. Its main task should be construction of a space station, plus repairing satellites. Its cargo bay ought to be of flexible dimensions, to accommodate space station modules of varying sizes, and it ought to have a short-mission capability, since three or four days is ample time to deliver parts.

NASA has contracted with Rockwell International for a fourth space shuttle without pausing to refine its mission. That is a blunder. A total, mission-oriented redesign of the fourth shuttle should have occurred with an eye to flying it in three or four years. The question is: What do we want the shuttle to do? If we want it to transport teachers, politicians and journalists, we can build an ultrasafe system, more like an airliner than a working spacecraft. But that's really not what we need. We need a space station.

NASA has already issued design requests for an orbital maneuvering vehicle (OMV), which would ferry parts and crew from the shuttle to the space station. I'd take the further step and build a space tug. Its design would pose fewer problems than we faced with the LEM, the lunar lander. The tug wouldn't be saddled with the weight constraints that were imposed by a lunar liftoff requirement. Like the LEM, though, it would not need to have an atmospheric re-entry capability, since it would not return to earth. The shuttle would refuel and resupply.

A few more thoughts about the tug. It would provide human comforts for crews—sleeping, eating and recreation facilities. It would be built to withstand radiation and able to sit in geosynchronous orbit—that is, stable in relation to earth. It would be equipped with robotic arms, similar to those on an underwater research craft. It wouldn't have to be pretty, just functional.

Once the redesigned shuttle and the tug are operational, we'll be ready to build a space station. When construction modules are delivered, a crew can be kept permanently in place—payload specialists to keep track of systems assembly, mission specialists to drive the tugs. With the station at about three hundred statute miles above the earth, it could be held in orbit by its own bank of thrusters or by being nudged by the tug. NASA has indicated that the station will be designed for twenty five years of use, but a thrust mechanism may be required to keep it there that long. I believed the Skylab would remain in orbit a lot longer than it did. It fell to earth, its orbits having decayed, because we didn't have the shuttle ready to keep it up there.

I'd like to see us develop a space station in which our men can feel their way. Today spaceflight is still in the experimental stage. We have yet to accomplish a real task up there. I define a task as doing work, bringing back a product that is worth more than the raw material we started with. To do that, we must first feel at home in the environment.

Our immediate objective over the next ten to fifteen years ought to be establishing the space station. Then we can proceed with missions to Mars, mining the asteroids and other great goals. But there we get into a twenty-five to fifty-year planning program. We should be careful to put first things first.

Enough of my being on a soap box. I've got stories to tell, and I suppose I'll have to run the risk of sounding self-centered.

Modesty may be a virtue, but it's not mine. My friend John Healey tells about a Chamber of Commerce lunch in my honor in Los Angeles in 1968. I had recently commanded the first Apollo mission, and Healey was the chief project engineer for North American Aviation, the spacecraft manufacturer. As my lengthy biography was being read, John gathered from my pained poses that I was uncomfortable. He was afraid I'd been offended and asked me about it later. I said, "I was trying to appear humble, but I guess I don't know how."

Humility is not a favorite trait in the world of air and space pilots. We place a premium on high performance—by man and machine. And we forgive a bit of boastful exaggeration. The dictionary defines a hotshot as a "showily skillful person." I accept that. It describes us quite well. Once we lose that gung-ho attitude, I maintain, it's time we turned in our wings.

There's a lot to be said for peer recognition. Looking back on my career as combat and test pilot and astronaut, I thrive on the esteem of my fellows. I'm happy to say that I belong to an old-boy network of astronauts and test pilots.

Fame is another matter. It wasn't until after I had flown in space that I realized I stood tall in the world. I was no longer an ordinary person. It didn't go to my head, I maintain, but I won't deny that I reveled in recognition. I remember going to Colorado in 1977 with my good friend and fellow astronaut Pete Conrad. Pete had done a television spot for American Express, the one about famous people who don't stand out in a crowd and who are identified when their name is typed on a credit card. As I was signing autographs during lunch one day, another friend wondered why I hadn't also appeared in an American Express commercial. "Oh, I'm too well known," I replied. Needless to say, Pete never quite forgave me, but we laugh about it still.

Until I flew in space, I'd had a devil of a time with my name. No one could pronounce it until they had got to know me well and listened as I drilled them: "Hurrah, Scheer-ah." A naval academy history instructor wondered if I was related to William L. Shirer, the authority on World War II in Europe. I didn't deny it and managed to pass the course. Jo, my wife, at one point began calling me Skyray—she still does, to tease me. I came to like it. Skyray sounds like Schirra, and it's the name of the F4D, the Navy fighter I first flew when I was a test pilot at Patuxent River, Maryland. Best of all it's a name everyone recognizes. I once used it as my CB radio call sign.

On July 1, 1986, I helped commemorate the seventy fifth anniversary of Navy flight by taking off in a PBY, a World War II patrol bomber, from Lake Keuka, near Hammondsport, New York. On that day in 1911 Lieutenant Theodore G. Ellyson, USN, flew from Lake Keuka for five minutes or so at about twenty five feet in a Curtiss A1. My role in the historic event involved flying a bomber, a seaplane yet. I'm a fighter pilot, and fighter pilots are particular. We avoid airborne delivery trucks, and we call seaplane pilots yoke boaters, alluding to the clumsy control mechanism of a flying boat, the yoke. I had been a yoke boater only once, when I was in flight school at Pensacola Florida, in 1948. But on this occasion, honored by the invitation to participate, I swallowed my pride.

From Hammondsport I went to New York City for the Statue of Liberty centennial celebration. There was a taxi strike, and people were milling on the streets. It was a happy and relaxed throng, and I enjoyed being part of it, though still feeling somewhat elevated. Not for long. I was in the Palm Court of the Plaza Hotel when this man approached. He appeared to be a typical New Yorker, brusque and to the point but well-meaning. He jabbed a forefinger in my chest, looked me in the eye, and said, "You used to be Wally Schirra."

Fame follows you in odd ways. In 1973 Jo and I built a home on the island of Kauai, in Hawaii. We were there not long ago, and I stopped by a real estate office in Princeville, the nearest town. I was interested in the latest land values.

I overheard an agent making a pitch to some people, and she said, "Here is where Wally Schirra's house is. You know, the famous astronaut." I looked at the map she was showing, and I noticed that she was pointing to an area far from where we lived, where property prices are well out of our range.

7

She kept repeating her mistake, and I finally could stand it no longer. I said to the woman, "That's not Wally Schirra's home. It's over there, on the other side of the map."

The woman was quite indignant. "Sir, I have been here for years, and I know where Wally Schirra lives."

"I'm awfully sorry, but that's not where Wally Schirra lives. Here is where he lives." I pointed to our neighborhood.

"Well, what makes you so sure?"

"I'm sorry ma'am. But you see, I used to be Wally Schirra."

2 Black-Shoe Navy: Annapolis to Tsingtao

My mother was Florence Shillito Leach, a Brooklyn girl. My father was from Philadelphia, the son of a world-famous cornetist, Adam Schirra, who had emigrated from Bavaria. Dad was also Walter Marty Schirra, Marty being the name of my Swiss grandmother. Of the original seven astronauts four of us were juniors. Psychologists have tried to make something of that—it's called "the incidence of juniorism in high-risk activity."

My parents met in 1916. Dad was a dashing aviator in Sam Browne belt and high leather boots. An engineering graduate of Columbia University, with Royal Canadian Air Force flight training, he was commissioned a first lieutenant in the U.S. Army Signal Corps. Dad often ribbed me about his jumping the rank of second lieutenant, aware that I was an ensign, the Navy equivalent, for three long years. He was an Army flying instructor in Corpus Christi, Texas, before going overseas in 1916 to fly for the RAF first, then for the U.S. Army, in 1917-18. He married my mother just before catching the troop ship. It was a whirlwind romance, as Jo's and mine would be thirty years later, only that Jo and I got married after I got home from the war.

Dad saw a lot of combat over France shooting down Germans, and on three occasions he was downed and listed as missing in action. His favorite story was about ferrying an aircraft from France to Britain at the end of the war. He asked a French mechanic what was in a box strapped to the fuselage, and the mechanic said it was something called a "parachutee." He'd flown without a parachute in combat, and when hit, he crashed the plane. Mother held two funerals for him and collected insurance money, which she returned. Dad came home healthy except for a hunk of shrapnel in his leg. To the end of his life he was unable to pass a metal detector test in an airport security check.

Dad's first job after the war was with the United Fruit Company, so he and Mom lived in Honduras for a few years. Then they settled in Oradell, a community in northern New Jersey, where Dad was the borough engineer. In the carefree days before my sister or I was born, my parents had a fine time barnstorming in a Curtiss Jenny. Mom was a wing-walker. With Dad at the controls she would dance on the lower wing of the biplane, using the struts for support. It looked hair-raising and no doubt was. Her act attracted customers who would pay five dollars for a turn around the field. When asked about it later, she would say she gave up wing-walking when I was in the hangar. So when old hotshots like Chuck Yeager or Scott Crossfield try one-upping me using their experience, I tell them I was flying before I was born.

Oradell was a small town, population about 2,100 then and now. The first American astronauts all came from out-of-the-way villages. Small-town values are a mark of distinction of the Project Mercury pilots. Respect for authority is a value that seems to diminish in proportion to the growth of a community. I grew up with a healthy respect for the men of the police and fire departments, and an early ambition was to be one of them. I respected my teachers too, and I remember the names of most of them.

Dad still flew during my childhood but just for the fun of it. He owned an Aeronca C3, and he took me up for the first time when I was eight or nine. I remember we climbed from the runway and headed into a stiff wind—it blew so hard that we were moving backward in relation to the ground. From that day on I loved flying. Teterboro Airport wasn't far from Oradell, and I remember riding there on my bicycle to watch the "airplanes." It wasn't until later that I learned an aircraft doesn't plane, as a boat does when it moves

10

through water. A wing generates lift passing through air, with the air on top going faster than air underneath, resulting in less pressure on top, thus lift. Aircraft were crafty vehicles, I thought, and I no longer called them airplanes.

I had a number of early heroes. One was Clarence Chamberlin, who crossed the Atlantic in June 1927, following Charles Lindbergh by only two weeks. I recall going for a ride with Chamberlin in a Curtiss Condor. I also watched Jimmy Doolittle—General James Doolittle, a hero of the war with Japan—fly a Gee Bee racer. I was in awe of a man in scarf, goggles and leather jacket. I wanted to grow into that image.

As a youngster I never met Lindbergh, but I could identify with him. I was four when he made his historic flight, and he lived for a few years afterward in nearby Englewood, the childhood home of his wife, Anne Morrow Lindbergh. I went to high school in Englewood, the Dwight W. Morrow High School, which was named for Mrs. Lindbergh's father, a former ambassador to Mexico.

Finally, in 1969, I met Lindbergh. As vice president of the Society of Experimental Test Pilots I wrote to ask if he wished to become an honorary fellow of the society. He had previously turned our offer down, so I advised him politely that we were extending it for the last time. He phoned me to say he'd accept, and he attended our dinner in Los Angeles in September. We met one month after the first landing on the moon.

I graduated from high school in 1940, in June, the month of the French surrender to Germany. Odd as it may seem, the war was not uppermost in my mind. I had my own interests; one of them was swing music. I was a fan of Glenn Miller, Harry James and Charlie Barnett. (Barnett, by the way, became a friend of Jo's and mine later on.) Frank Sinatra sang at one of my high school dances. Following my grandfather's footsteps, who performed with the Philadelphia Symphony, I was trying to master the trumpet. Surprisingly, quite a few astronauts were musically trained. Deke Slayton, like me, played the trumpet, John Glenn the trombone, Scott Carpenter the guitar, and so on.

I was also an automobile nut. First I bought a part interest in an old Ford, a Model T. Then I had a sporty Pontiac with a rumble seat. My favorite was a 1932 Plymouth roadster with side curtains and wire wheels. I paid thirty five dollars for it in 1941.

11

One evening I was tinkering under the hood of my Plymouth, adjusting the carburetor, and I noticed that the engine was moving in relation to the frame. I called my father, thinking the engine was loose. He gave me a short lesson in basic engineering, pointing out that the engine mounts were made of rubber. It was my introduction to "floating power," as advertising people call it.

Dad had a good friend, a neighbor named Jack Glindsman, Uncle Jack to me. A senior mechanic of a New York City automobile company, Uncle Jack often brought home brand new model "exoticars," such as the British Lagonda. Dad once asked Uncle Jack to help him tune and service his Chrysler Airflow. Uncle Jack said the car should be steam cleaned, and he appeared a while later in a white smock and examined the car with a doctor's stethoscope. It taught me something about technicians.

Uncle Jack was the first of three technicians I have known who exemplified the value of vocational training. The second was a chief petty officer with whom I served in the Navy. The third was Guenter Wendt, who was in charge of preparing our spacecraft for launch. On a Navy ship 90 percent of the crew is vocationally trained opposed to college educated.

No, I didn't know war was coming. My attention was focused on going to college, dating young women and keeping my Plymouth running. I wasn't unusual. Staying out of the war was a major issue of the 1940 election. When the Japanese bombed Pearl Harbor on December 7, 1941, lots of people were surprised. I was then a student at Newark College of Engineering, and on Monday, December 8, students in the Reserve Officers Training Corps came to class in uniform. I suddenly was aware of a national emergency.

Dad wanted me to go to West Point, and I agreed with him to the extent that a military education would be a quick ticket to a career in aviation. In the fall of 1940 I had entered the engineering school in Newark, New Jersey. The purpose was to cram for exams that would determine if I qualified for an appointment to the military academy. When I took the exams, I filled in a block at the top of the form with the letters USMA. I took a number of tests in math and science, feeling I'd done pretty well. Then a proctor announced that those applying for the military academy should remain for the history test. I raised my hand and asked if I might make a change on the application form, which he granted. I carefully substituted the letter N for M, making my academy designation USNA, and went on my merry way.

Shortly thereafter Dad appeared at the door of my fraternity house at Newark College, clutching a telegram and beaming.

"Congratulations," he said. "You've been accepted. But there's been a slight mistake. It says naval academy."

"It's not a mistake, Dad. I changed my mind at the last minute."

My father was disappointed, but he respected my decision. If the truth were told I really hadn't made it on the spur of the moment. As a young kid I had watched a Navy aviator walking down the street in Oradell, his green uniform, the sharp gold wings above his left pocket, and his polished brown shoes shiny. From that day on I always wanted to go to Navy.

My three years at Annapolis have largely disappeared in blurred memory. I was in the class of 1946, but wartime acceleration enabled us to graduate in 1945. A five-year program was crammed into three, leaving me with impressions but few details forty years later.

I do remember a midshipman in my company—I was a company commander—who stole examinations and sold them. He had not been caught, but word got around, and we decided to apply our own kind of justice, the silent treatment. He would not be spoken to or even recognized—he was no one, as far as the corps of midshipmen was concerned. He lasted a month and resigned from the academy.

The naval academy though had its happy side. My warmest memories are of Commander Harry Bean Jarrett, whom we called Uncle Beanie. A younger officer who had been with the fleet and had returned to serve on the faculty, he inspected our quarters, parading through in full-dress uniform. But the formality of his dress disguised a man sympathetic to the nuances of the human condition. Once Uncle Beanie discovered a midshipman was making nightly journeys through a utility tunnel. He followed his wayward sailor one night and caught him making love to a woman who worked in the laundry. What to do? Like Solomon, Uncle Beanie made a wise decision that we forever loved him for. A discipline report was filed. The offense: "Unauthorized articles in a laundry bag."

After graduation from Annapolis I learned that a congressional investigation had determined that the class of 1946 was full of draft dodgers. The congressmen had charged that some of my classmates hoped to avoid combat. As a matter of fact, the war in Europe had ended by the time we graduated, and the Japanese capitulated within a few months. So we saw only limited action.

True, many men in my class left the Navy soon after graduation. Chuck Blackford, my roommate, was one of them, going on to be a successful banker. But in my opinion draft-dodging was a bum rap. I believe those who left simply saw little future in a postwar naval career and decided against it.

There was an incident at Annapolis that I'd rather not remember. As a company commander I carried a sword in dress formations, using it to salute as we passed in review. The salute took a bit of skill and a lot of practice. I carried the sword in my right hand with the tip of the blade touching my right shoulder. To salute, I whipped the blade up in front of my nose, then down to my side. Right arm stretched and elbow locked, I would be holding the sword in front of me, with the blade tip pointing at the ground.

I always feared that I'd blow this tricky maneuver. One day it happened. I'd been issued a sword that was too long. I carried the tip too low, and it stuck in the dirt. I had no choice but to march on, trusting the retrieval of my sword to someone following in the ranks.

I've made many trips to Annapolis since my graduation. The most memorable was in April 1981, when all of the naval academy astronauts returned to review the corps of midshipmen. After the parade we were standing on the steps of Bancroft Hall with the superintendent, Vice Admiral William Lawrence, a Vietnam war hero. I'd known Bill Lawrence when we were both test pilots. The battalion commanders and their staffs were passing, saluting with their swords. One midshipman staff officer was a woman who must have been five-foot-five, no taller. Her sword was too long, as mine had been years before, and when it hit hard pavement, there was a reverberating clang that made me shudder. But history didn't repeat. She managed to retrieve the sword, catching it on the bounce.

WAR AND MARRIAGE

The sea Navy is black-shoe; the air Navy is brown-shoe—the distinction is important to us. In the air Navy we wear brown shoes with our greens and khakis, black shoes only with our blues. We also call any ship on which we have made an arrested landing, meaning an aircraft carrier, a boat, which infuriates the fleet Navy. To them a boat is a small craft that can be carried aboard a ship. And we are aviators, not pilots, for pilots are civilian people who bring big boats into harbors. That notion of course riles our friends in the Air Force.

I was black-shoe Navy from the time I joined the Pacific fleet in the summer of 1945 until I began flight training in 1947. I had requested cruiser duty and was assigned to *Alaska,* an armored cruiser. It's never *The Alaska*, just *Alaska*. Dropping "the" before ship names was probably adapted from the British style, as are many Navy traditions. *Alaska* class ships were new to the Navy. They were designed to counter a reported vessel the Japanese were building, an improved version of the German *Deutschland* class pocket battleship. The reports were incorrect, but *Alaska* went to the Pacific anyway, arriving at Pearl Harbor in January 1945.

Upon graduation I went to visit my parents, who now lived in Arlington, Virginia. As an Annapolis graduate and a Virginia resident, I was a member of the Army-Navy Country Club. One day I went to the club for a swim, and I noticed a willowy blonde gal sitting by the pool. She was really pretty. She was sitting alone wearing a bikini. I made up my mind to meet her. I asked a few of my poolmates who this stunning woman might be, but no one knew. I noticed that she was getting up, perhaps to leave. I couldn't lose her and I rushed over and said, "Hi, I'm sorry, but nobody seems to know you. I'm Wally Schirra."

Her name was Josephine, or Jo, Fraser. Born in Seattle, she lived there until her father died and her mother remarried, when Jo was 13. She then moved first to China and then to Washington with her mother and stepfather, who was a naval officer. I asked her to dance at the club that evening, and she said okay, though a bit tentatively. I was on cloud nine, and had there been a cloud ten or eleven, I'd have been on them too.

Now this is a story Jo loves. We got to the dance, and she had me waltz her over to this older couple, who turned out to be her mother and stepfather, William T. Kenny, a Navy captain. To a fresh-caught ensign wet behind the ears a captain was a god, a superior being. I was trying to collect myself when the band began to play a bebop tune, and Jo asked if I'd like to jitterbug. I said I'd rather not. I was in uniform, after all—we were always in uniform in wartime—and I didn't think it would be proper. But Captain Kenny asked his wife to jitterbug and off they went. That was the last time I ever declined to jitterbug with Jo.

I courted Jo for seven days. That's right—seven days. You have to remember that this was war, and like my Annapolis experience everything was compressed. We didn't have much time to learn about each other, but we got the essentials. We were both Episcopalians and both left-handed. We were also about the same age, Jo being a year and two weeks younger. There were differences too. As a Navy junior Jo had traveled widely—to China, Australia, Tahiti, Hawaii—while I had gone from New Jersey to Annapolis to Arlington. It was only after I had flown in space that I could say I'd been to more places than she had.

The war was in full tilt, and I expected to be gone for a long time, so I told her I'd write every day via FPO San Francisco. I was determined to marry Jo. She was still tentative, understandably, but I was convinced I'd come to know her well. I learned that her aloofness, while showing her to be sophisticated and intelligent, concealed her warmth. I realized she was shy. I realized we loved each other.

I was right in pressing my case. Jo and I have been married for forty-two years.

I reported to *Alaska* in July 1945 in Buckner Bay, Okinawa, a Seventh Fleet staging area. The ship had seen a lot of action in seven months—at Iwo Jima and Okinawa and in the bombardment of the Japanese home islands. I came aboard carrying a Bowie-like knife made for me by a fencing instructor at Annapolis, planning, I suppose, to engage the Japs in hand-to-hand combat.

I expected the war to be drawn out by the Japanese—a series of costly landings against a determined enemy. Then suddenly, in August 1945, it was over. We heard reports of the A-bomb being dropped—at Hiroshima on August 6 and at Nagasaki on August 9—but an incident that occurred in the time between those awesome events kept us on war alert. I was standing on the fantail of *Alaska* when *Pennsylvania*, a battleship anchored nearby, was hit amidships by a kamikaze.

Another reason it took us a while to realize the war had ended was the primitive state of radio communications. There was no worldwide satellite net, so transmissions were not instantaneous. The news trickled out via the F network or foxnet, which was operated by bouncing signals off the E-layer, an ionized layer of the atmosphere sixty to seventy miles up. The E-layer is also called the ionosphere. The signals return to earth in a random way, and if a radio receiver is in the right place, it will receive them.

We were still using the E-layer technique at the start of the space program, in Project Mercury, although our transmitters and receivers were more precisely positioned. I might note too that in spaceflight we create our own ionosphere when we re-enter the atmosphere. The ionization of molecules around the spacecraft causes a brief communications blackout. On the early spaceflights it was a period of anxiety for people on earth.

The atomic bombs dropped on Japan in 1945 inspire more serious thoughts. They were the only nuclear weapons ever put to use. In my twenty-seven years of military service I never handled a nuclear weapon, never even saw one. There are tens of thousands of them in our arsenal. When I was at the China Lake test center, I had a special clearance, called a queen clearance, because I worked with nuclear delivery systems, attack aircraft. Sometimes at night at China Lake, in the California desert, I could see flashes of light from the nuclear range over the mountains in Nevada.

Boosters that sent me into space, the Atlas and Titan, were designed to carry warheads. Still, I don't consider myself a nuclear warrior.

In the fall of 1945 *Alaska* made a show of force in the Yellow Sea—up to Korea and back down to China—and we docked at Tsingtao, a Chinese city known today for its beer. Two other ensigns and I went on liberty in Tsingtao. We rented saddle horses from a Russian who lived there and went riding in the surrounding hills. When you leave a city in China, you're in open country in a hurry, but pretty soon we came to a settlement, or so it appeared to be. It was actually a Japanese Army fort still on wartime alert. I first realized that when I saw the Japanese flag being lowered. It dawned on me that we had been taken for an American military patrol sent to accept the surrender of the garrison. We looked the part, I suppose, as we were dressed in khakis and cloth caps called piss-cutters.

We were scared silly, to be honest, but we weren't about to let it show. One of our party was a couple of months senior in rank, so he accepted the sword of the commander of the fort. We gave it to the skipper of *Alaska*, Captain Kenneth Noble. I'd picked up a souvenir, a Nambu 9 millimeter pistol, and I'd talked a U.S. Marine into selling me a Japanese motorcycle and sidecar for about fifty dollars. I brought it back lashed to the afterdeck of *Alaska*.

We returned to the U.S. on *Alaska*—to the east coast via the Panama Canal—with a skeleton crew. Many of our officers and men had gone home, having qualified for separation under the point system. One day I was ordered by our acting skipper, Commander James Grant, to exercise the number-two gun turret. I hadn't been trained as a gun officer, so I was about to learn from experience on an operational battle cruiser.

I went below and called a meeting of the chief petty officers. I admitted I was in trouble and needed their help. I got it and was able to carry out the assignment. I had remembered the advice of an old sailor who taught seamanship at Annapolis. "If you ever need help in a hurry," he said, "go to your chief." I was again reminded of the value of vocational training.

I got back from the war in December 1945. *Alaska* was berthed at Staten Island, New York, and I took a train to Washington, where I was met by my father, my sister, Georgia, and Jo Fraser. I had told Jo in a letter that I intended to marry her. She may not have been fully convinced, but I pressed the point, and we were wed on February 23. We moved into a garage apartment on Staten Island, and Jo insisted that I sell my Japanese motorcycle. It's not that she was fearful. God knows she had married the wrong guy if she was worried about high-risk vehicle accidents. Jo just didn't like noisy motorcycles and still doesn't. Besides, we needed the money, and I got ninety dollars for it.

YOUNG CHINA HAND

Alaska was mothballed within a month or so of our getting settled in the apartment, and I was assigned to the staff of the commander of the Seventh Fleet, Admiral Charles Maynard Cooke. Headquarters was a communications ship, *Estes*, tied up at Tsingtao of all places. So I flew back to China, and Jo followed by ship once orders were cut for her to accompany me.

Jo had lived in China when her stepfather Bill Kenny was stationed in Shanghai. In 1941, when war between the U.S. and Japan was imminent, Captain Kenny was assigned to the staff of Admiral Ernest J. King, the fleet commander, and Jo, her mother and her sister were evacuated and sent home. In 1946, a family reunion occurred. Jo was with me and her mother and stepfather were in Nanking, the Chinese capital. Captain Kenny was the naval attaché to George C. Marshall, the ambassador to China and former Army chief of staff. Nanking was a short airplane ride from Tsingtao. In fact, we once went to visit the Kenny's on General Marshall's plane. Here I was, still an ensign, surrounded by stars. Marshall was a five-star, Admiral Cooke was a four-star, and the chief of staff, Rear Admiral Fred Boone, was a two-star.

I was a briefing officer, responsible for keeping Admiral Cooke and his staff up to speed on a range of subjects, particularly the movement of typhoons and their predicted effect on Seventh Fleet operations throughout the Pacific. There were no satellites to afford a peek from space, but data from ships at sea gave us a pretty good plot. On one particular typhoon, though, some Buddhist monks told us the storm would hit Wangpoo harbor in Shanghai dead-on. Our scientific evidence indicted otherwise. So we ignored the monks, even though their prediction was based on centuries of observation. To my chagrin the monks were right. So much for modern science.

I also briefed Admiral Cooke of the status of supplies arriving in Shanghai as a part of a United Nations relief program for China. Predictably, a shipment would be reduced by half to theft before it could be warehoused, and much of what remained would be stolen as it was carried by navy ship—smaller ships as the cargo load was decreased—up the Yangtze River to Chungking.

I was learning about the hard realities of world trade. It's not honorable in the way that former President Jimmy Carter— Annapolis, class of 1947, and in the company I commanded—thinks it ought to be. Kumshaw and baksheesh are understood in all languages to be the stuff that greases the palm of the hand you do business with. I witnessed the loss of our cargos en route to Chungking, knowing that theft was but one crime of many the traders committed. Such swindles date back to the Phonecians.

I also watched the Communists overrun China. A high crime rate in the neighborhood in which Jo and I lived—practically a robbery a night—was an expression of revolutionary contempt for the American "imperialists." As a protective measure we practiced with small arms in our back yard. The Nationalist population, fleeing the Red onslaught, swarmed into overcrowded Tsingtao. They were desperate for money, for food or a passage to freedom, and they sold their valuable possessions for a song.

It was just a year after the end of the second great war, and the world was heating up again. A well-trained military man has reason to fear war. That's because we don't play war, we do war! The bell wasn't ringing, yet, but it was tinkling. I knew when we left that China would never be the same again.

A Wish Fulfilled

I was the first member of my academy class to enter flight training. Thanks to Admiral Boone, an aviator himself, who urged me to get into aviation. Later I would single out impressive youngsters and try to recruit them. It's an unwritten tradition of the Navy, brown-shoe or black-shoe. An up-and coming officer becomes a protégé. His name is listed in something like a little black book.

I had three sponsors, and oddly enough they all were named Tom—Tom Moorer, Tom Connolly and Tom Walker. When I arrived at China Lake, I reported to Moorer, then a commander and the experimental officer. I told him of my disappointment at not being sent to the Naval Air Test Center at Patuxent, Maryland. I wanted to be a test pilot. "Son," he said, "you're here to develop a new weapon." It turned out to be the Sidewinder air-to-air missle, a weapon still in the Navy inventory. During my stint at China Lake, from 1951 to 1953, Connolly and Walker, both commanders and career naval aviators, succeeded Moorer. (When the F14, a Grumman fighter called the Tomcat, came along in the late 1970's, each of the Tom's claimed it was named for him.)

In early 1969, as I was retiring from the Navy, I went to Washington to receive the U.S. Navy Distinguished Service Medal. Tom Moorer was chief of a naval operations then, and Jo and I stayed at his quarters on the Naval Observatory grounds. "You're hearing shipping-over music, Schirra," said Jo—recruiting music, the song they play when they hope you'll sign on for another tour of duty—as we unpacked. Sure enough, the next day all three Tom's ganged up on me, and it was an impressive array—Moorer a four star admiral, Connolly and Walker both three stars. I was offered command of the test station at China Lake, where we had all served, and probably a promotion to the rank of rear admiral.

I was tempted, but finally I said no. I wasn't prepared for such a command, even though I had been given heavy responsibilities, such as a $500 million space flight. Also, I hadn't been to staff school, so I lacked the experience other Naval officers expect. Before I made my final decision I sought the advice of James E. Holloway, Jr., a retired admiral, who was Jo's second stepfather. Holloway had married Jo's mother following the death of Bill Kenny in the mid-1950's. He had commanded *Iowa*, a battleship, in World War II, and in 1958 he became commander in chief of naval forces in the eastern Atlantic and the Mediterranean. Admiral Holloway was a man of action who

20

showed his stuff in the Lebanon crisis of 1958, and he was a man who didn't mince words. His reaction to the possibility of my going to China Lake was typical: "You'd be a potted palm."

3 Brown-Shoe Navy: The Making of a Hotshot

THE LUCK OF THE DRAW

I got my wings in June 1948 and reported to my first fighter squadron, VF71, at Quonset Point, Rhode Island. Joe was with me when we arrived late on a Friday afternoon just in time for happy hour. I went to the Officers Club and asked for the commanding officer, Armistead Burwell Smith. I was directed to a corner of the room where Commander Smith was standing on his head drinking a martini. Later in the space program, I was grateful to "Chick" Smith—who became a lifelong friend—because he demonstrated a man could take fluids at negative one gravity. When doctors raised questions about our ability to drink in weightlessness, at zero gravity, I told them about the upside-down commander.

Flight training lasted nearly two years, beginning in Dallas in 1947. Jo watched me solo in a biplane called Yellow Peril. I continued my training at several Navy havens—Corpus Christi, Texas, Pensacola, Florida, Jacksonville, Florida, and then back to Pensacola. I was checked out for carrier landings with the SNJ, a Navy trainer, and my first fighter was the F6F, the Grumman Hellcat.

There was one fortuitous event during training—in fact, I consider it a major turning point. Having just learned to fly, but before being assigned an aircraft type, I arrived at a window along with another student, Pinky Howard, who was a year ahead of me at Annapolis and had been promoted to Lieutenant junior grade. The woman at the window said she had one fighter billet and one seaplane billet, and we would have to draw straws. Howard said hell no—he was a j.g., and I was an ensign. The woman responded with that old saw about rank between ensigns and j.g.s being like virginity among whores and told us to draw. Howard got the short straw and became a yoke-boater—the term is derived from the lever or yoke that is used to control a flying boat. I got fighters; Pinky resigned a few years later.

On June 10, 1948, just before I received orders to Quonset Point, I was designated naval aviator J1362. Four days before there had been another big event. I was promoted, having been an ensign for three years to the day. That was par for the course in those postwar years, but it seemed a long haul.

In VF71 I flew the F8F, which was and is my favorite airplane. One of the Grumman series, all named for pussy cats—F4F Wildcat, F6F Hellcat, F8F Bearcat, F9F2 Panther, F9F6 Cougar, F11F Tiger, F14F Tomcat—the F8F is not a plane you climb into; rather you strap it on, which is one reason it is so exciting to fly. I did not fly the F8F in combat. By the time the Korean war came along, I was flying jets. In fact, the F8F was never deployed in wartime by a U.S. force, although it was flown in Vietnam by the South Vietnamese.

Fond as I was of the F8F, I lost of number of good friends in the squadron, especially after we went from the F8F1 to the F8F2. The F8F2 had an automatic fuel mixture control, very similar to an automatic choke on an automobile, that often caused the engine to sputter and quit in the carrier landing pattern. If an F8F dropped into the ocean, recovery of the pilot was all but impossible, because he was trapped in the cockpit.

I went on a couple of Mediterranean deployments with the F8F. (I'm careful to call them deployments, not cruises, because the idea of our cruising the Med doesn't sit well with Navy wives.) The fact that my first squadron skipper was a bona fide fighter ace—Chick Smith was credited with 10.5 Japanese planes in World War II—made the deployments great training exercises. Smith was replaced by Al Rothenberg, who'd flown PBY's in World War II. I thought it was heresy to have a yoke-boater as the CO of a figher outfit, but it turned out I was being unfair to Rothenberg, who was an outstanding leader. He was tough, but he cared about the welfare of his boys.

My favorite story involving Al happened one day when I was up in an F8F at Quonset Point for gunnery runs, firing a 20-millimeter cannon at a towed sleeve. I thought I was getting to be a darn good flyboy, so I would cruise alongside the sleeve to see how many hits I'd made. I could put my canopy almost against it and make out the color left by the painted tips of my rounds. But then I came into land, the first in a flight of four, and I got caught in a turbulence caused by a P2V, a multi-engine Lockheed Neptune, that was landing in front of me. My F8F flipped, and I found myself flying upside-down two feet off the runway. This was a dumb place to be, I said to myself, so I hit the throttle and pushed the stick forward. My aircraft climbed up and rolled out, as if I had planned it that way, which was what Rothenberg was thinking as he watched from the ground.

Actually I was scared almost senseless, but I had been able to maneuver to safety on instinct. It's like blinking when you're about to be hit in the face. You react to an emergency by doing what's required to save your life. In this test, obviously, there is an ultimate failing grade.

As I landed and taxied to my slot, Rothenberg was waiting for me. He was a lieutenant commander and the skipper, and he was really chewing my ass. I was just a lieutenant j.g., but I ignored him as I climbed out of the plane. I got down on my hands and knees and kissed the ground.

"What the hell are you doing?" Rothenberg demanded.

"I'm just glad to be alive," I replied.

In 1988 I got a call from John Brannon, a retired Navy aviator who was my wingman in VF71. "Do you remember me?" he asked. "Of course," I replied. "Turn on your TV set to Channel 10," he said. I did. It was a boxing bout, and there was Al Rothenberg. He'd been a boxer himself and now was a referee.

OUT OF THE PACK

My first jet training was in the Air Force F80, the Lockheed Shooting Star, when I went to a transition school at Pensacola. When I returned to the squadron, I had a close escape in an F8F due to the difference in jet-powered and propeller-powered aircraft. In a jet you don't use much rudder. There is not much torque in the engine, so you simply aim the aircraft, and it looks like you're sailing along a wire. In a propeller plane you must kick a lot of rudder to compensate for engine torque. I forgot this basic rule on my first F8F takeoff after jet school and almost crashed.

In 1949 Squadron VF71 got a new skipper, John Starr Hill, who would come over the horizon again in the Apollo program. We also made a transition to the F9F2 Grumman Panther. It was the Navy's first operational jet fighter.

Up to this point Grumman had been the major supplier of Navy fighters, but McDonnell, North American and Douglas were moving into positon to compete. In those earlier one-digit airplanes we used the second letter to designate the manufacturer—Grumman was F (F8F), McDonnell was H (F2H), Douglas was D (A4D), and Lockheed was V (P2V). But when we got into two digits, as with the F14, we dropped the manufacturer's digit designation. We used just funny numbers, as we long had accused the Air Force of doing.

Just to confuse the issue completely, there is the case of the Air Force F80. As a Navy trainer, the type I flew at Pensacola, it became the TV1 (one-seater) and TV2 (two-seater). The Air Force training version is the T33, also known as the T-bird.

In the early summer of 1950 we were with the Sixth Fleet in the Mediterranean on our first deployment with the F9F2. We were aboard the aircraft carrier *Midway,* accompanied by another carrier with a squadron flying the F2H Banshee, a McDonnell jet fighter. A few fellows in that squadron, I knew, had been selected to serve in the Air Force in an exchange program. The idea was for junior officers to swap careers for a year, to learn how it's done in the other service. Then, when these officers reached the level of joint commands, they'd know how to communicate with each other.

The Korean war started on June 25, 1950, while we were on deployment. We returned to Quonset Point, but the other carrier was ordered straight to the Far East. I realized that the officers in the Banshee squadron would not be able to fill the exchange billets. I saw my opportunity to become a combat pilot with the Air Force in Korea, and I seized it.

I flew to the headquarters of COMAIRLANT (Commander, Naval Aviation Forces, Atlantic) in Norfolk, Virginia, and announced I was available for the exchange program. I also proposed a fellow volunteer, Alfred "Ace" O'Neal. I wanted a combat assignment, but

I was also seeking to avoid the training command. None of us looked forward to teaching cadets who might get us killed, nor did we relish the idea of flying those dinky SNJs again. We wanted to go higher, farther and faster—in the newest jets. If the first astronauts were superachievers, we got that way as military fliers.

When I got back to Quonset Point, I called Ace O'Neal. "We made it," I said. "They've got you on the list too." We were ordered to report immediately to the Pentagon in Washington for a briefing on the exchange.

Here comes sneaky Schirra again. I had a good friend, Slade Nash, a West Pointer who was an Air Force captain assigned to headquarters at the Pentagon. Nash told me about a National Guard wing from Arkansas—it was a P51 unit scheduled to transition to jets and go to Korea—that was being transfered to Langley Air Force Base in Hampton, Virginia. Ace O'Neal was assigned to an F86 squadron, and I envied him, for the F86 was a hot airplane. (As it turned out, Ace spent his exchange tour at Otis Air Force Base, not far from Quonset Point, in Rhode Island.) I joined the Arkansas National Guard wing at Langley.

In retrospect I can see this was the point in my career when I started to move out of the pack. I was climbing the ziggurat that Tom Wolfe talks about in *The Right Stuff.* By being selected for the Air Force exchange, I was one of twenty Navy aviators who would be noticed. When I got to Langley, I learned that only the wing commander, a colonel, had ever been in a jet. He had been up for all of one hour in the back seat of a T33. We were due to fly the F84 Thunderjet, a fighter-bomber built by Republic. So I got checked out in the F84 and then helped train the rest of the wing. Two months later we were flying missions in Korea—all the way north to Pyongyang, the North Korean capital—from Itazuke Air Force Base in Japan.

KOREA, 1951-52

It was an arduous trip—by train across the United States and then by transport from Travis Air Force Base in California—to Itazuke. We were put in officers' quarters, cottages with double-decker bunks out on a porch. I remember thinking about the situation that first night as I drifted into deep sleep. The last time I had thought about Japan was in 1945, when I was in Okinawa in combat. Now Japan was our ally.

I slept in skivvies under a sheet and awoke to see a woman standing next to my bunk, a maid. Call it culture shock or just plain modesty, but I stayed put for two hours until she finished her work.

We were in Japan for only a short time. It was a long flight to our targets—across the Straits of Tsushima over the South Korean port of Pusan, then north to the 38th Parallel—and we were returning to our base on the fumes of depleted fuel.

In a month or so the wing was moved to a base in South Korea, called K2 and located at Taegu. I had gained a lot of respect for the pilots in the Air Guard wing. They were all command pilots, meaning they wore wings with a star and wreath to show their senior status. It offended them at first when I called the wreath a toilet seat, but they soon understood my sense of humor.

I envied anyone who had flown the P51. It was a hot airplane that had been designed by an engineer at North American, Harrison Storms, whom I would come to know well. Storms was later the chief engineer for North American on the X15 rocket plane program of the National Aeronautics and Space Administration. And when North American got the contract with NASA to build the Apollo lunar spacecraft, Storms again would be named to oversee the project.

I made ninety combat flights in Korea over eight months, and I shot down two Migs. Our main mission was air to ground—to bomb enemy installations and transport facilities, usually railroads. At first, when we saw the North Korean Mig 15s coming at us, we pickled our bombs, we dropped them indiscriminately, so we'd be lighter and more able to fight. The North Korean pilots, having watched us waste our bombs, figured their job was accomplished and shoved off. After that we kept our bombs at least until the Migs were in range. One time I pulled out of an attack on a locomotive and saw two Koreans firing at me. That made me mad, so I came roaring back and strafed the machine gun pit. I didn't know if I got them, but I felt better. Then I realized how dumb it was to waste my airplane and my training just to shoot back at a couple of guys on the ground.

I was developing a sense of values, even if at times they were in conflict with my basic motivations.

Occasionally I'd draw an assignment that would lead to a direct engagement with the Migs, such as covering B29s on bombing runs over North Korea. When the Migs attacked—flights of Migs were referred to over our radios as trains—they'd seem to be all over the place. We had offshore radar, based on an island whose location was highly classified, that could pick up the Migs coming off the ground. We would listen to reports of two trains here, three trains there, and so on.

On this day the Migs had effectively tied up our F86s and were about to make it very hectic for those of us in F84s and for British pilots flying Gloucester Meteors at our side. I spotted a Mig coming up from beneath a B29, blazing away, and I nailed him. I did not make a classic fighter maneuver. He was slow, and I was above him—in the right place at the right time. But I was looking, and that's the art of being. It was my first Mig.

I was elated, but I tried not to let the thrill of victory interfere with my defensive senses. The best part was getting back to the base. I was this hotshot Navy kid with a Mig to my credit, telling the Air Force I was back. I buzzed the airport as low as I could get and pulled up to do an Immelmann on top of an Immelmann. (An Immelmann is a half-loop maneuver named for Max Immelmann, a German aviator in World War I.) I pulled up from the second half of the loop with barely enough air speed to avoid stalling, when two Air Force pilots in T33s each made a pass on me. They ruined my show, as we say, but it was fun just the same.

The Base commander, a colonel named Red Mason, upbraided me for buzzing the field. My smirk made him all the more angry. "Keep it up," he warned, "and I'll ground you." The showoff stuff is officially prohibited, but warriors have engaged in it since the days of jousting knights.

The Mig was a tough adversary, even for the F86, which was more of a match for it. There were times in the F84 when, outclassed, we'd be forced to drop to a lower altitude. The F84 is a straight-wing aircraft, and down low swept-wing aerodynamics are of no great advantage. So we could turn inside the Migs or at least turn with them. Often they would not like what was happening and just climb away. On a couple of occasions I got to use Navy maneuvers, and the Mig pilots were so surprised to see a Navy tactic in an Air Force airplane that they said bye-bye. They were sharp, though. They knew our tactics.

I got my second Mig in a direct confrontation. The air was saturated, and we were badly outnumbered. It's amazing how well we did on days like that. It was discipline more than anything else. We realized we didn't have to give up. We got over the intuitive fear of seeing a gun fired at us, learning to deny that we'd be hit.

A story was told of combat troops, when I was at the naval academy. The sergeant said to his platoon that out of thirty men, only two would be alive on the following day, whereupon each man turned to the other and said, "I'm sorry for you pal." It's sublime faith, and once you learn that it's dumb faith, you're too smart to be in combat.

Fatalism is an important ingredient of the combat attitude. So is ignorance in the same sense that you're unaware of how awful it can be. I have witnessed death, but in an impersonal way—an airplane went down, but I did not see the pilot in agony. Same way when I've had a close call. I was once hit by antiaircraft flak, and it left a big hole in the wing of my F84. I was a bit startled, but I didn't dwell on the problem. I realized later that if the impact had been four feet to the left, it would have ruined my day.

Four friends were shot down in Korea, and only one was recovered. He was rescued from a mudflat by a seaplane and taken to the island where the secret radar was operating. He was sent home pronto, because it was dangerous for him to know about that island. I had watched as the seaplane picked him up, after I strafed the scene to prevent his being captured by North Korean soldiers.

As for the friends who were killed, I followed a simple rule. You wear a black arm band, mentally if not literally, for a reasonable period of time. Then you take it off. You don't dwell on the loss.

How a human being adapts to the rigors of combat is something to think about. Some guys go dingaling. The rest of us go through a strenuous testing time. For the early astronauts who had fought—Glenn, Grissom and I flew in Korea, and Glenn and Slayton saw action in Europe in World War II—it was a big plus to have survived with our sanity intact. No one knows how a guy will react until he is tested. Mock combat—like the Navy's Top Gun program in San Diego, for example—is useful, but it's altogether different when he's up against someone who really wants to kill him.

I did mock combat before Korea and after. Before Korea I'd maneuver against another aviator, a friend, until one of us made a kill. Then we'd break off and do it again. After I'd returned from Korea, if I got on a guy's tail, I'd say, "You're dead. We don't need to go through it again." I wasn't playing games any longer; I was determined to prevail.

In the days before Korea I was impressed by an F8F squadron flier who got so low that he dipped his propeller in the ocean. It was like teenagers playing guts with their cars. A test of courage. I had passed the test flying in combat and was no longer impressed with games. This attitude stuck with me throughout the space program. My rambunctious approach to the off-duty aspect of life may have fooled some people, but this is not a game, I often said to myself. This is for real.

There was a lighter side to the tour in Korea. At the base in Taegu we had barracks without partitions. Someone discovered sheets of plywood stored in an unsecured supply building near our quarters. So we organized a series of midnight requisitions for plywood. We also found tools and nails, and we built comfortable rooms for ourselves. Years later I ran into the base commander—the same Red Mason who had chewed me out for buzzing the field after shooting down my first Mig—and learned we had been conned. If Mason had ordered us to partition the barracks, we'd have told him to shove it. So he put the plywood in a place where we could steal it, thinking we were putting one over on him.

There was one Korean mission that left me angry. I had a Mig dead to rights, when my wingman came through loud and clear: ''Break right.'' Now, when you get that message, you don't discuss it. It means that whatever you're doing, forget it, and get into the hardest high-G turn you can make to the right. And it usually means an enemy aircraft is right on your ass about to shoot you down. So, wham! I broke right, still unable to figure out why. Then my wingman came back on the radio: ''Yalu River. You can't cross the river.''

This was my first experience with the rules of engagement. President Truman fired General MacArthur over carrying the war from North Korea into China. But that's my point. Rules of engagement are political rules. Politicians toss them around—rather blithely, I think. Military men don't understand them and aren't supposed to. It's like telling a prize fighter who has his opponent on the ropes ready to knock him out: ''Don't hit.''

Of course I broke off. Had I pursued that Mig across the Yalu, I would have been court-martialed, and my Navy career would have ended then and there.

CHINA LAKE, 1952-54

I was a lieutenant during my Korean hitch. Advance in rank was slow during those years of an excess of military manpower. We kept waiting for our tubes to come, so named because promotion notices were sent out in tubular cardboard containers. It was at the Naval Ordnance Test Station at China Lake in California that I finally made lieutenant permanent. In December 1951 I had arrived in Washington by train, as I had when I returned from World War II, but this time there was no big celebration, no foofaraw. Jo was at Union Station, of course, and she had our eighteen month-old son, Marty, in tow. I told Jo we were headed for China Lake.

I was annoyed at first at being detailed to weapons testing. My aim was to be a real test pilot, which meant going through the Navy school at Patuxent River in Maryland. I soon became aware, however, that an airplane was part of a weapons system. Without a weapon you can fly pretty sky patterns and lay smoke screens, but that's about it.

The prospect of becoming a west coast aviator pleased me. There is keen competition between the east coast Navy and the west coast Navy. East coast loyalists were irritated, for example, when the movie *Top Gun* glorified the training school at Miramar in San Diego. Although I was born and raised in New Jersey, I had shifted my loyalty to the west coast. I got along well with the guys out there, other Navy aviators.

Throughout my career I have inched my way westward—from Langley Air Force Base in Virginia, to Houston and Denver, and finally to Rancho Santa Fe in Southern California, where I now live. I had wanted to return permanently to California since being assigned there in the 1950's.

In our first meeting Commander Moorer asked if I had any complaints as a recently returned Korean war hotshot.

I replied, "My weapons were lousy." I explained I had been armed with .50-caliber machine guns, and they had a low impact energy. I said I had camera footage to prove I'd have shot down another Mig, my third, with an effective weapon such as a rocket.

Moorer walked me across the street from his office to a large complex of test laboratories. A couple of Ph.D. types were in a room, and they had a dome-shaped device, made of glass, that would fit on the end of a five-inch HPAG (high performance air to ground) rocket.

Inside the dome was a small optical device, a manmade eyeball. I was a cigarette smoker in those days, and I had one in my hand. As I crossed the room, I noticed that the eyeball was tracking me, or my cigarette to be precise. I realized it was a heat-seeker.

"This is your new toy," said Moorer. As an air-to-air missle it would be called Sidewinder, after the desert snake. I was to be the project officer.

I had fooled around with primitive rockets in Korea. Our F84s at Taegu were equipped with JATO bottles, for jet assisted takeoff, but I had decided we could get off without them. One day, as we were flying with the JATO still strapped on, the Migs showed up. As they dove down on us, I radioed to my three buddies, "Light JATOs now." As the bottles ignited, they laid streams of smoke behind us. The Migs left in a hurry. It wasn't much of a rocket flight—that is, the JATOs had little effect on our air speed. However, our secret weapon scared the wits out of those North Korean pilots, who'd never seen anything like it.

When I got to China Lake, I told how I had used the JATO, and a rocket expert said I was lucky to be alive because those bottles could easily have exploded in a cold temperature, and at 25,000 feet it's about minus fifty degrees. I found how dumb I had been. In developing the Sidewinder, we were hard put to make it suitable for air-to-air combat at high altitude. (Years later rocket engineers still hadn't learned to appreciate the effects of temperature—witness the *Challenger* accident.)

The HPAG had been introduced in World War II as a solid rocket fired in a random manner—that is to say, unguided— from an aircraft at a target on the ground. When they designed the Sidewinder, they took the HPAG and added canards to the front—four tiny triangular wings that afford maximum mobility. The canards were designed as part of the guidance package, and they were placed up front near the package, so it wouldn't be necessary to run wires the length of the rocket. (Canards were also used to steer *Voyager*, the aircraft flown nonstop around the world in 1987 by Dick Rutan and Jeana Yeager.)

I was the first pilot to fly with the Sidewinder. I was an engineering pilot though, not a test pilot. That came later when I got my doctorate, so to speak, at the test pilot school at Patuxent River. When I was a test pilot, I flew the first F4H, the McDonnell Phantom.

Now this is the sort of story I like to tell, as I look back on my career as a Navy aviator. In Vietnam in the early 1970s there was a Navy ace, Commander Randy Cunningham, who shot down 5 Mig 17s. He was firing the Sidewinder from the F4H—"my" weapon and "my" airplane. There will be a Randy Cunningham exhibit at the San Diego Air and Space Museum, and it will feature an F4H, the actual one Randy flew, A sidewinder, and a Mig 17.

I got to fly a slew of airplanes at China Lake. The F86 Sabre was one, and I thought it was about time, having watched this swept-wing job with envy while I was in Korea. Others were the F3D and F84F, a swept-wing version of the F84 I flew in Korea, and a series of ADs— AD1, AD2, AD3, AD4—which were piston-slappers built by Douglas. I might also have flown a twin-engine prop plane, possibly a Beechcraft, but it's not recorded. Fighter pilots are particular about what they list in their log books.

I fired the Sidewinder for the first time, a dummy with no explosive charge, from an AD4. We used piston-engine planes in the beginning because their slower speed made it easier to track moving targets. I was able to hear the tonal signal, an audio sound produced by the heat of the target, as the optical device sought it. A visual readout of the signal is shaped like the letter M, and the center of the M is the node. When the node is on target, you launch, and the homing device literally sees the infared image of the target and goes for it. Once launched, the Sidewinder is on its own.

We worked on another missile, called OMAR—Optically Maneuvered Aircraft Rocket—designed to find its way to the target by following the track created by the illumination. OMAR never went into production, but the technique was applied to later generations of weapons.

I also spent some useful time at China Lake learning about ground-to-air missiles, the ones aviators worry about. One was the Terrier, but my buddy Tom Amen and I called it "the admiral seeker."

Amen was another hotshot doing test flights at China Lake. As a Navy aviator in Korea, he had downed three Migs. He was senior to me, a lieutenant commander, but we shared a desk and lots of jokes. Tom was later killed in a crash. It was one of those unnecessary events. He wasn't testing an aircraft, although he was a test pilot. He was just going somewhere, I think in a Beechcraft. He was a fourth Tom—

along with Moorer, Connolly and Walker—and I would have liked to see his career run its full course.

Amen and I were called on to act as guides when VIPs came to China Lake to watch a Terrier launching. On one occasion we escorted a senior admiral from Washington and a civilian bigwig, possibly the Secretary of the Navy. Those details are fuzzy, but what happened is not.

The Terrier went straight up and did a hammerhead, an inadvertent flip that sent the missile straight back down. We stood there and watched, increasingly aware that it would hit nearby and possibly in our midst. The dignitaries were busy digging holes or ducking under what little protection there was. They looked pretty foolish. Tom Amen and I just stood there, knowing there was nothing we could do. It made no sense to dive for cover and then to die, if the missile did hit, with your butt in the air. I was reminded of a saying: "He who has his ear to the ground has his ass exposed."

Amen and I had no fear of disaster. We shared the fighter pilot's fatalism. It grows on you in training, or at least it ought to. Otherwise, you're bound to let fear get the better of you. I've seen it with carrier pilots—they lost their nerve and were forced to quit. I'm talking about a pre-screening process. If I hadn't been through it as a fighter pilot and a test pilot, I might not have made it as an astronaut. I had a couple of hairy moments in the space program—a bad roll by the Atlas booster during the Mercury launch and a false liftoff on my Gemini flight, but I was ready.

It's difficult to predict who will stand up under pressure. We had one fellow in the F84 squadron, who was Jack Armstrong, the All-American boy, and another who was Casper Milktoast. Quite a contrast. Jack Armstrong was built like a halfback, good looking, loud-mouthed—a real hotshot while we were in training. Milktoast was a wimp, to use the modern terminology. But when we got to Korea, Milktoast was the best damn fighter pilot in the squadron, and Jack Armstrong peeled off his wings after two missions. (An interesting parallel when one considers the politics of 1988.)

Danny Balmer was Mr. Milktoast, and he really looked the part— small, frail, soft-spoken. But Danny was a tiger in combat. He was sitting on the runway at our base in Taegu one day, getting ready to take off with JATO bottles and two 500-pound bombs aboard (our F84Es were classified as fighter bombers). Suddenly his engine blew, as those Allisons frequently did, and Balmer, who was sitting on a full load of fuel, knew it was time to make a hasty exit. He climbed out of the cockpit and ran along the wing. As he did, his .50-caliber machine guns began firing, triggered by the heat of the engine fire. A sergeant in a nearby tent was slightly injured in a fall that was caused by a machine gun round hitting the leg of his stool. The only other casualty was Balmer, who broke an arm or a leg when he fell off the wing.

I was airborne when all this happened, but I heard the details later. We relished the story for a long time, especially the last part. The machine gun fire also shredded stockings and underwear hung out to dry by female Red Cross personnel. My buddies and I were delighted, because we'd been scorned by these woman. They had refused to give the time of day to anyone below the rank of a colonel.

SAN DIEGO, 1954

After two years at China Lake I was a weapons expert and assigned to an evaluation group at Miramar Air Naval Station in San Diego. Our job was to test the Cutlass, the F7U3, a twin-engine fighter built by Chance Vought. The company soon became Chancy Vought to us, for in our judgement the Cutlass was an accident looking for a place to happen, a widow-maker.

The Cutlass hadn't yet been delivered to a unit, and our group formed the framework of a squadron. A senior project officer was Don Shelton, who was a year ahead of me at Annapolis and today is a retired rear admiral and a close friend. Shelton was a graduate of the test pilot school at Patuxent, as was another project officer, Floyd Nugent. I was one of five fleet pilots who rounded out the group of seven and next to the bottom in rank.

Chance Vought—the company became Ling Temco Vought, now LTV, based in Dallas—later made good airplanes, such as the F8U Crusader, a supersonic (Mach 1.5) day fighter. The Cutlass test project can be justified as a learning exercise. It taught the Navy delta wing aerodynamics, and it gave us valuable experience with afterburners.

The afterburner is an augmented thrust device that is of optimal benefit on takeoff and at velocities higher than Mach 1, the speed of sound. To say the Cutlass is supersonic is stretching a point. If you put it in a perfectly smooth dive at 35,000 feet—you cannot yaw even slightly—you might pass through Mach 1.

Now for the bad news. The Cutlass has leading edge slats, and if the plane stalls with its slats in, it's not recoverable. It's called a post-stall gyration. If you're at low speed with slats out, you can come down like an elevator, beautifully. But if the slats are in, the plane goes into wild and random motions. There is then but one recovery technique. You eject.

We noted this in a report rejecting the Cutlass, but it didn't discourage the people who wanted to see it go into production, including politicians.

We did a test with the Cutlass on *Hancock*, an aircraft carrier, in which Floyd Nugent took off using a steam catapult. He did a series of catapult takeoffs—takeoff, come around, and do an arrested landing—and because of special equipment for the test he couldn't retract his landing gear. He was barely airborne, with the nose of the Cutlass way up high, looking like a praying mantis, when his nose wheel dropped into the sea.

Nugent couldn't land, and we went through agony trying to decide what to do. I was helpless, flying around the carrier in another Cutlass. Running low on fuel, I landed at Miramar.

It was decided to have Nugent eject. He had the airplane headed just right, so it would fly over the town of Coronado, across the bay from San Diego, and crash in the ocean. Then he ejected, landing safely on North Island, where Coronado is located. But as he looked up, Nugent was shocked to discover that the Cutlass was maintaining a perfect circular course. When he ejected, his canopy and seat had come out too, and the weight reduction had altered the trim just enough to put the airplane on a level flight path.

The Cutlass flew for another half hour or so, though it seemed like an eternity. It circled the stately Del Coronado Hotel, and we wondered if we should recommend evacuation. We also considered ways to shoot the plane down, but none seemed feasible. Finally the Cutlass made a perfect landing right off the beach in fifteen feet of water. Had it not been for salt-water corrosion, it would have been in condition to fly.

The Cutlass was declared operational, which I viewed as a mistake. It would account for several fatalities before it was finally grounded. Four members of our group formed a Cutlass squadron at Miramar, and three of us—Don Shelton, Burt Shepard and I— went to Moffett Naval Air Station near San Francisco to train other Navy aviators on the plane we had tried to reject.

SCHIRRA'S SPACE

SAN FRANCISCO, 1954-55
We joined VC3, a training squadron at NAS Moffett, on the south end of San Francisco Bay. We were the F7U3 Cutlass team of a transitional training unit. There were three other teams in the unit. Bob Baldwin, a graduate of the naval academy and TPS Patuxent, and today a retired vice admiral, led a team that trained on the FJ3 Fury, the Navy version of the F86. We also had teams on the F9F6 Grumman Cougar and F2H2 McDonnell Banshee, and since we crosstrained, I got to fly all of the TTU aircraft. I no longer flew only the damn Cutlass.

In overall charge of the TTU was a senior test pilot, H. G. "Bud" Sickel, Jr. J. D. "Jig Dog" Ramage was the VC3 commander. J. D. no doubt had a fit when according to a new Navy alphabet his name was changed to Juliet Delta.

TTU was designed to train key personnel of squadrons scheduled to take the various aircraft to sea—the commanding officer, executive officer, operations officer and maintenance officer. I believe the TTU was the prototype of the Top Gun program at Miramar. Our objective was to train fleet aviators in air combat techniques by simulating combat situations, teaching them how to use their fighter aircraft to the optimum and instilling the idea that they were the hottest guys in the air. That's what Top Gun is all about.

There was an F86D unit at Hamilton Air Force Base, on the north end of the bay, and as we flew over a mountain east of Berkeley, called Diablo, we would radio, "Diablo three zero," meaning we were at 30,000 feet, plus or minus 10,000, requesting combat. It was eyeball combat—we were dueling with a mock enemy we could see, not a blip on a radar screen. It was combat for real, not golly-gee stuff. We had some pretty good hassles.

We learned tactical maneuvers as we taught them. For example, I devised a way to use the slats on the Cutlass at high altitude and avoid a stall by flying at a low indicated air speed. Then I'd hit the afterburners and turn inside my opponent. If I got on his tail, I'd scored a kill, so we'd break off. This kind of training is dangerous, high-risk work. But we didn't press it too far. I was good at it, because I was combat trained. People who weren't combat trained tended to go a loop too far. My job was to teach them their limits.

The executive officer of the TTU was R. W. "Duke" Windsor. He was a test pilot and is a friend to this day. We like to laugh together

38

and outdo each other in the practical joke department, and it began at Moffett. One Sunday, for example, Duke and I and two others went on a jaunt to Dallas to check out an airplane being designed by Chance Vought. "Wheels up at 0900," Duke had declared, and we took him at his word. When he was a half-hour late at the airport, we had a hydraulic jenny and jacks under his Grumman Cougar, lifting its landing gear off the ground.

Here's my favorite Duke Windsor story. Two of us in the TTU, Bud Sickel and I, had been on Air Force exchange, logging a lot more flight time than we would have in the Navy. In the Air Force they stay in the air longer, not so mindful of the need for a fuel reserve. With carrier landings you don't dare run low on fuel, because if you miss on an approach without a reserve, you've lost your airplane and maybe your life. Bud Sickel had over a thousand hours in jets, the first Navy pilot to reach that mark, and I was ten hours short of a thousand.

Duke Windsor was also approaching a thousand hours in jets, and as exec of the TTU he had the authority to ground me.

"You can't fly for a while, Schirra," he said. "You need some time off."

So, sneaky Schirra rides again. I went across the field, to an instrument training school. They flew the T33, or the Navy version of the Lockheed trainer, the TV2. Windsor was so busy flying that he never missed me, and when I reported back in a few days, I had nine hours on the T-bird, legitimate jet hours, and only one to go. I went to Windsor and pleaded.

"Duke, I've got to stay current on the F9F6 Cougar. We have a new class coming in." "Okay," he said. "You can take her for one hop." So, I shoved off, and when I landed, I had my thousand hours; plus some supersonic time.

That afternoon Duke took off in a Fury despite lousy weather, resolved to make his milestone. Sickel and I were there to greet him when he landed, and we had a big sign that read: "Welcome to the thousand-hour jet set."

Windsor never quite forgave me, though our friendship survived. He retired as a captain when prevented by diabetes from making admiral. He moved to Houston, where he and Al Shepard became business partners. Windsor's late wife was a Coors heiress, so he and Al owned a Coors beer franchise.

I was in good company at Moffett. It was a congregating point for the Pacific Fleet's top aviators—the hotshots of Navy aviation, I'd say, knowing Al Shepard, an east coast pilot, would take exception. I was lucky enough to be flying alongside test pilots, guys who had been to the school at Patuxent River—Shelton, Baldwin, Sickel, Windsor. There was also Tom Connolly, one of the three Toms, and Red Dog Davis—both Connolly and Davis are retired vice admirals. Bob Elder, who later was my air group commander, had come to the Navy via a college training program for regular officers, as opposed to reservists. (Called the Holloway Plan, it had been formulated by Admiral Holloway, Jo's stepfather, when he was chief of naval personnel in the 1950s.)

When it was finally time for me to go to TPS Patuxent, these guys all threw in happiness chits, recommendations. There's an old saying about the cream rising to the top. That certainly applies to naval aviation. Everyone above the rank of lieutenant commander knows everyone else. Not because we went to college together. I didn't know of any of these guys at Annapolis.

I'm grateful for these friendships and more than grateful when I realize that my close colleagues from Navy test pilot days show a high survival rate. All are alive today except Bud Sickel, who died in 1959. He was flying an FJ3 when he was asphyxiated by an oxygen mask malfunction.

I had not met Al Shepard yet. He was a year senior to me, class of 1945 at the naval academy, although we had many mutual friends. Don Shelton and Bob Baldwin were Al's classmates at Annapolis. Nor had I yet encountered any of the future astronauts. While I might have heard of a hotshot marine who had made a celebrated cross-country fight and appeared on a national TV quiz show, I hadn't met John Glenn.

In fact, I didn't know much outside my little world. I can recall where I lived in those years, but I was so wrapped up in aviation I didn't think of anything else. Jo tells a story of a hurricane that blew into Florida when we were there. When the big wind hit, according to Jo's bittersweet memory, we flew our airplanes to safety and left our families behind.

Fortunately, she understood the Navy and stuck with me even though I was incorrigible. I didn't even know the popular songs of the period, not to mention movies. As for world events, I paid no attention.

I checked out Po Harwell in the Cutlass at NAS Moffett. His name was Paul O. Harwell, but he was Po always. He would be one class ahead of me at TPS Patuxent, and our paths would again cross when I was the commander of Apollo 7, in 1967. Po was then an in-house astronaut for North American, the spacecraft manufacturer, as was John Starr Hill, who had been the CO of VF71, my first squadron. Their job was to sit in for the Apollo crew during spacecraft tests.

Po and I took off in formation, both in a Cutlass, and I flying to his right rear. The Cutlass is a single-seater, and this was next best to being in a seat behind him. I was in position to tell him if something was wrong and how to deal with it. Essentially, I was walking him through the flight.

Right after takeoff I noticed that an engine was aflame, burning violently. I radioed, "Po, shut down your port engine." He thought this was part of the routine, although engine shutdown at five hundred feet must have seemed somewhat unusual. "Okay, if you say so, boss," Po replied uneasily. By then the aircraft was engulfed in flames, and I commanded, this time with urgency, "Po, shut down your starboard engine and eject." He remained calm and said, "I don't remember hearing about this maneuver in ground school." Harwell ejected. Within seconds an explosion destroyed the aircraft. Po parachuted safely into San Francisco Bay, but he injured his arm because he was wearing an expandable metal watchstrap. I noted that, and I never wore that kind of watchstrap or any type of bracelet afterwards.

We record flight time in the Navy in tenths of hours, rounded off to the nearest six minutes. With that one flight Po Harwell flew one tenth of an hour in a Cutlass—he correctly blamed the crash on an aircraft malfunction—and two tenths of an hour in a parachute. He never flew a Cutlass again.

While I was still with VC3 at NAS Moffett, a new fighter was delivered to the TTU, the F3H McDonnell Demon, and our team was assigned to it. The Cutlass was being phased out of service, much to our relief. The Demon was a night fighter, an all-weather aircraft, with sophisticated radar that would indicate the azimuth and range of a target. Don Shelton was one of the early night fighter pilots. He had flown instrument missions in the F6F, the Grumman Hellcat, although not in combat. I had been a day fighter, so in order to get checked out on the F3H, I went to the McDonnell plant in St. Louis.

Dave Lewis was project officer on the Demon and later president of McDonnell Aircraft. The founder of McDonnell, James S. McDonnell, Jr.—as an astronaut I would come to know him as Mr. Mac—took personal pride in the Demon, precursor of the F4H, the Phantom II, McDonnell's most famous warplane. I came to realize how important it was to be familiar with the internal structure of the aircraft industry and to understand the competitive maneuvering of the corporate world. Industry people—engineers and executives—made decisions upon which my life depended. In the space program this became an even greater reality.

Dave Lewis eventually had a falling out with Mr. Mac and resigned from McDonnell, the prime contractor for the spacecraft in the Mercury and Gemini programs. He joined General Dynamics—the Convair Division of General Dynamics built the Atlas, the Mercury booster—and became chairman of the board.

SAN DIEGO, 1955-57

We trained a team to replace us as instructors on the F3H at Moffett, and we returned to Miramar in San Diego to form an F3H squadron, VF124. We had a bad beginning. Our skipper, Shannon McCrary, crashed and died in the mountains east of Miramar on an instrument approach. Our executive officer, Shorty Ewing, had an engine flameout and slid down the runway in a fireball. Ewing lived, but he was so badly burned he had to turn in his wings. Paul Payne, a veteran flier and a Patuxent graduate, became our commanding officer, Shelton was made exec, and I was the operations officer.

I argued that an all-weather fighter should be flown in all kinds of weather, blue as well as black, and in day and night both. Payne and Shelton were night pilots, Ed Porter and I—Porter was another test pilot and our engineering officer—were day pilots. We developed an all-weather, day-night training cycle, and we crosstrained, so the four of us got experience in all conditions.

We deployed to the Far East aboard the carrier *Lexington*, with Bob Elder as the commander of Air Group 7. It was my first opportunity to put the Sidewinder to an operational test. I got the F3H modified to fire the missile, and then I went to China Lake to obtain missiles. The Sidewinder was such a new weapon that there was no allocation procedure, and I had to pull strings.

We were the first fighter squadron to fire a Sidewinder. We used a Regulus missile as a drone, a target, and Shelton got the first kill. He, Payne and I were all in the air at once, flying different courses. Shelton just picked the Regulus up on his radar, slid in, and blew it to shreds. "You goofed that one, Schirra," said Shelton, when we got back to the carrier. I gave the credit to his radar, and we've kidded about it ever since.

We returned to San Diego, and I spent four months in late 1957 attending aviation safety school at the University of Southern California. The university administers the course for all of the military services. The experience was a plus, and I have Paul Payne, my skipper, to thank, because it was his idea. It got me into gear again academically, for one thing. And it taught me a lesson that would serve me well in the space program. In the investigation of an accident the principal objective is to prevent a recurrence.

PATUXENT RIVER, 1958

I had been flying for nearly ten years in the Navy, and it was apparent that I was due for shore duty. My luck was still holding, however. I had avoided the training command, and I was a candidate for test pilot school. I applied for TPS—officially it's called the Naval Air Test Center at Patuxent River, Maryland—and was accepted. I reported to Pax River in January 1958.

I think of going to test pilot school as part two of the story called "Coming out of the Pack." I had started coming out of the pack in the Air Force exchange tour. The second coming was test pilot school. I was in class 20, by now optimistic about my future in the Navy.

Test pilot school was a "go" all the way. I flew late-model aircraft— F4D Douglas Skyray, F11F Grumman Tiger, F8U Chance Vought Crusader, F3H McDonnell Demon—but not the latest. That came later. It was a tough course, particularly the ground school. I had to learn math all over again, and like everyone I struggled with supersonic aerodynamics. Some guys, seven of a class of twenty-six, were there for the academics only. They were specialists in one of the test divisions—flight test, service test, armament test and electronics test. I would become a specialist after graduation.

As experienced pilots—I guess by this time I had stopped insisting on being called an aviator—we learned a specialized way of flying. We flew set patterns and applied certain techniques, all for the purpose of producing data points for engineers to study. We worked on a high-speed maneuver, a high-acceleration maneuver, a turning maneuver. And we flew by the letters—paying strict attention to preset speeds for takeoff, cruising and landing.

We also learned how to communicate with engineers. This was the most valuable asset that I took from test pilot school to the space program. We wrote reports on our flights, reducing the data in a way an engineer would appreciate. A written report was required for each flight, and it typically took hours to write. We also learned how to communicate one on one, from one specialized breed to another—we talked about tactical maneuvers and power settings and whatever else was of mutual interest. We would log data points, which would be the basis for charts that others would fly by.

TPS Patuxent was familiar territory and not just because the base is fifty miles down the Chesapeake shore from Annapolis. Three of my flyboy buddies from California, Don Shelton, Bob Baldwin and Bud Sickel, had returned as instructors. And I got to know a good bunch of fellow students, some of whom would be joining me in the space program. Jim Lovell and Pete Conrad were both members of Class 20, and Dick Gordon had been in class 19. Lovell, Conrad and Gordon joined the space program in the second and third astronaut selections, and all flew in the Gemini and Apollo programs.

Lovell was named the outstanding member of our class. He worked his butt off, though, and Conrad and I, who tied for second, ribbed him for not enjoying life. Patuxent was a great place for outdoor sports like water skiing and sailing. We also had a lot of fun kidding each other. One of our classmates, Bruce Sheasby of the Royal Canadian Air Force, weighed all of 105 pounds. We called him Two Slug, because a slug is a unit of mass that weighs 32.2 pounds. Sheasby was later killed on a test flight. He was one of several class members to die in the line of duty.

Jim Lovell, Pete Conrad and I are still close today. That's to be expected, I believe, since we lived through test pilot school and the space program together. I think of Navy aviation and manned spaceflight as ultimate peer programs. For one good reason—you depend on your peers in a life and death business. Yes, we are very careful when we rate each other.

I graduated in the fall of 1958 and was assigned to Patuxent as a full-fledged test pilot. In October I went to Edwards Air Force Base in California to test the F4H Phantom II. Built by McDonnell, the F4H was a much improved version of the F3H Demon, the aircraft I had recently taken to sea.

I had decided to specialize in service test despite an effort by Bob Elder, my former air group commander, to sign me up for flight test. The F4H had been flight tested, both by McDonnell and by the Navy. According to procedure a company test pilot flies it first, and a Navy pilot takes it from there. Dick Gordon was one of the Navy test pilots on the F4H. There were no newer airplanes coming along, so I figured I could make a greater contribution service testing the F4H. Service test is to determine if the airplane is suitable to the Navy's needs. Will it fit on a carrier? Can it be maintained according to specifications? I went a step further. I married the F4H to the Sidewinder. My fighter plane and my missile made a complete weapons system.

This was a period of firsts in my life. The F4H is a Mach 2 airplane, so for the first time I traveled at twice the speed of sound. The F4H I flew was the first off the line, the first of over three thousand planes to be built. But, again, a sad note. The McDonnell test pilot who checked me out to fly the F4H at Edwards, Zeke Huelsbeck, later died in a crash of that very same plane.

One evening at Patuxent, as we were about to graduate, I was writing a report on an aircraft I had tested, the F4D, which would do Mach 1 on a level course in ideal conditions. Someone called me outside and pointed to the sky. It was dusk, and there was still enough sunlight to illuminate a moving object. I knew immediately it was the Soviet Sputnik, which had been launched a year earlier. I wondered why I was messing around with an airplane that could barely make Mach 1, when a Russian satellite did Mach 25. It was one of the few times until then that I had given any thought to going into space myself.

In February 1959, just when my future seemed to be falling into place, I received blind orders, (meaning no reason was given) to report to Washington. I was one of several Navy officers, all fliers, to get them. It turned out that they went to Air Force and Marine pilots as well. Don Shelton and Bob Baldwin got orders, as did their Annapolis classmate Al Shepard, who was a staff officer in Norfolk. John Glenn, assigned to the Pentagon, was also on the list.

The suspense lasted until the day I reported to the Pentagon along with thirty or forty fellow officers. We learned we were candidates for a program of the National Aeronautics and Space Administration to send a man into space. The program had been named Project Mercury.

I didn't want to go, because it meant leaving the Navy. I wanted to be cycled back to the fleet with the F4H, get credit or take blame for its performance, and put it through its paces as a tactical fighter. I saw myself as the first commander of an F4H squadron. The space program to me was a career interruption. Others felt the same way, and some declined to compete. Po Harwell was one. And some of my friends—I'm talking about Don Shelton and Bob Baldwin—didn't make the first cut. That disturbed me. I accepted the challenge but with great reluctance. It was a tough decision—for me and for others. Pete Conrad and Dick Gordon would later shuck their Navy careers, having actually gone to the fleet with the F4H.

It had to do with being the first or the only—first man in space, first to land on the moon, whatever. Since I was the only astronaut to fly in Mercury, Gemini and Apollo, I believe I made the right decision.

4

My Ultimate Peer Group

Early in the preflight phase of the Mercury program the original seven astronauts sought a briefing on the X15, a rocket plane built by North American and being tested by NASA at Edwards Air Force Base in California. The X15 pilots were crucial, for they had flown in near-space, where aerodynamics are absent and an aircraft's flight path can't be changed with ailerons, elevators and rudder. To maneuver at altitudes above fifty miles, a pilot must use a reaction control system consisting of tiny rocket engines, or thrusters.

We wanted to learn from Scott Crossfield, who made the first X15 flight, and the others about the basics of spaceflight. What techniques had they developed? How had they practiced in a flight simulator? We intended to pick up where the X15 pilots had left off. They saw it differently. We had not flown in space, they had, and we were never going to catch up with them. I still don't understand how test pilots like Crossfield could have believed that nonsense.

Some observers at the time maintained the X15 could go into orbit. They totally disregarded an obvious hazard—the aircraft did not have the external surface to withstand the heat of re-entry into the earth's

47

atmosphere. It would burn up. Such intelligent people were letting their enthusiasm blur their sense of reality. The Air Force had a project called DynaSoar, a manned space glider being built by Boeing. But DynaSoar also did not have a heat-resistant surface and would have disintegrated on re-entry.

The Mercury man-in-space program faced competition, we soon realized, and at times it would get bitter.

Before we went to Edwards I called Forrest S. "Pete" Petersen, now a retired vice admiral and then a Navy test pilot. He had been an instructor when I was at Patuxent and then had joined the X15 program. I asked Pete about the protocol, better known as the drill, and he put it bluntly: "You'll be snubbed." Sure enough, Scott Crossfield and the rest wouldn't give us the time of day. I was somewhat taken aback, but I understood. We were being treated as space heroes—on the cover of *Life* and so forth—before we had gotten off the ground. Professional jealousy was to be expected. After thirty years, though, I count the X15 pilots, Crossfield in particular, among my closest friends.

Let me jump ahead, and then I'll fill in the details. In September 1987 I attended the annual meeting of the Society of Experimental Test Pilots (SETP) in Los Angeles. A number of X15 pilots were there—Scott Crossfield, Pete Knight, Jim Wood. At the opening reception Crossfield was introducing Jeana Yeager. Jeana is technically not a test pilot, but she had made the nonstop flight around the world in *Voyager* with Dick Rutan, who is a test pilot and a member of SETP. Jeana was a newcomer, and Scotty was trying to make her feel comfortable. That's Crossfield today.

Scotty is one of the certified pioneers of aviation. Besides being the first to fly the X15 he was the first to break Mach 2, twice the speed of sound. He has often been confused—by Tom Wolfe, for example—with Chuck Yeager, who never flew the X15. Chuck Yeager, who isn't related to Jeana Yeager, studiously ignored the epic flight of *Voyager*, which was ungracious of him. I say hooray for *Voyager*, but I like to remind Jeana and Dick—any my friend Burt Rutan, who designed the plane—that they orbited earth from east to west, which to an astronaut is the wrong way around.

At the peak of his career Crossfield made a mistake. He quit his job with NASA to become a test pilot for North American. Scotty believed he could earn a better salary and still fly the rocket plane. However, it doesn't work that way. Too bad, he was told, but he was a contractor pilot. Military and NASA pilots would fly the X15, and he would monitor their tests.

Scotty hadn't analyzed the situation thoroughly. Early in the development of an aircraft, not at the stage the X15 had reached in the mid-1960s, there is a place for a company test pilot. He looks over the shoulders of engineers, as they draw up a design and begin to cut metal. He makes recommendations—say, on the configuration of the cockpit display panels or on the control system. And he's the one who rolls the plane out of the hangar and displays it to an array of applauding executives. He's their hero, their financial future. Finally, he's cheered by an audience of admirals and generals and civilian bigwigs from the Department of Defense.

There comes a time, however, when the routine gets boring. Test after test is performed to determine the flight envelope of the aircraft, the three-dimensional curve within which it can be flown, as defined by its parameters, or limits, in speed, altitude and acceleration. When we talk about extending the envelope—I tried to explain this to Tom Wolfe but failed—we are referring to a process of plotting data by which we expand the area of the curve. Once the company test pilot has established an envelope, a customer test pilot—he could be military or he could work for NASA—takes over. He validates the flight tests and performs others—the service, weapons and electronics tests. The company test pilot is out of the picture.

The X15, Mercury, Gemini and Apollo programs were never boring, and there was an important procedural difference as well. NASA pilots, not company pilots, flew in the development phase. Crossfield must have understood this, having flown the X15 as a NASA pilot. Yet as a pilot for North American, the contractor for the Apollo spacecraft, he tried to get involved in the man-in-space program. He applied in 1967, soon after the Apollo 1 fire in which Gus Grissom, Ed White and Roger Chaffee died. I was in charge of the accident investigation and scheduled to command the first Apollo flight. Unfortunately I was the one to tell Scotty there was no slot for him.

Crossfield had a rough go for a while, but he landed on his feet. He went to Florida and worked for Eastern Airlines, whose president was later Frank Borman, a former Air Force test pilot and astronaut. Scotty then went to Washington, replacing Jack Swigert, another ex-astronaut. Swigert was staff director of the House Committee on Science and Technology until 1982, when Jack ran for Congress from his native state of Colorado.

Colorado had been my home since the early 1970s, and I campaigned for Swigert. He joined the space program in 1966, having flown in the Air Force and as a test pilot for Lockheed, and he was the command module pilot on Apollo 13. He left NASA in 1973. There was a hiatus between the last Apollo flight and the start of the space shuttle, and he preferred to take charge of the staff of the House committee, whose chairman was Olin E. "Tiger" Teague, a Texas Democrat and avid supporter of the space program. Then Jack ran for Congress, as a Republican, and he won. Unfortunately, before he was sworn in he died of cancer.

Yes, there's an old-boy network of test pilots, I'm happy to say. I was reminded of it over and over when I was at the SETP meeting in Los Angeles in September 1987. There was Scott Crossfield, talk about closing the loop. Now we are on excellent terms. I called Scotty when I was in Washington as a director of Kimberly Clark. An airline owned by the corporation, Midwest Express, was the subject of an investigation by the National Transportation Safety Board because of a fatal accident. The NTSB concluded pilot error, even though there had been an engine explosion. I needed an engine expert in a hurry, and Scotty produced one.

I also saw Don Segner at the L.A. meeting. Segner, who was in the class just ahead of me at test pilot school, is a Marine and probably the best helicopter pilot in the United States, if not the world. When we were at Patuxent, we were neighbors, and we each had a Vespa motor scooter. We would ride off together in the morning in scooter formation.

When Ronald Reagan ran for president in 1980, I spoke on his behalf in the western states—Colorado, Wyoming, Montana and Idaho. So I later got calls from President Reagan's people, wondering if I would come to Washington—as an official of NASA, the Navy, or the Department of the Interior. I said no thanks, because Jo and I were strongly opposed to an eastward move. We had made it to Colorado, and it was California or bust. But I saw an opportunity to do Don Segner a good turn. I had never lost my admiration for Don, so I said that I had a friend who would fit neatly into the new administration. Don ended up in the number-two spot at the Federal

Aviation Administration. The top guy at FAA, Don Engen, is also a former test pilot and a retired vice admiral. I chatted with Engen's wife as we were leaving the SETP meeting—we we were waiting for our cars to be brought from the hotel parking garage. "Don is considering the job at the Department of Transportation, replacing Mrs. Dole," she said. "If he takes it, I'll kill him." Like Jo and me the Engens wanted no more of Washington.

I was a member of SETP before I joined the space program, for I had been an active test pilot. I was its vice president in 1969-70 and was supposed to be a candidate for president in 1971. However, I had just started my own business, an environmental company in Denver, and couldn't devote the time the presidency required. Bob Hoover had been president in 1969, and he agreed to serve again in 1971. I consider Bob, a former test pilot for North American and a Navy TPS graduate, the world's best stunt pilot. He was Yeager's backup on the first flight of the X1, and in 1988 he was inducted into the National Aviation Hall of Fame.

Thanks to Bob, whom I met when I was at China Lake and he was doing test flights at Edwards, I became a fellow of the society in 1971. You progress from member to associate fellow to fellow. That is the highest honor in our profession—to be named a fellow.

Al Shepard is a fellow; John Glenn is not. As for other Mercury astronauts—Deke Slayton is a fellow, but Gordon Cooper and Scott Carpenter didn't make it. Gus Grissom, who is deceased, is not a member. Tom Stafford, my Gemini co-pilot, is a fellow, as is Pete Conrad. Jim McDivitt, who commanded Apollo 9 on a lunar orbital flight, is a fellow, and so is Neil Armstrong, the first man to walk on the moon. A fellow is accepted by those who have already made it, about fifty of us in all, and a single negative vote amounts to rejection. That's why I call the society my ultimate peer group.

A fellow has to have done some good stuff, some exemplary test flights. He's an out-of-the-pack type. When a test pilot becomes a fellow, he has reached the peak of his career.

I look at a list of fellows of the society, and I know just about all of them. It's not as amazing as it might seem, since they're all from my era. Take Bob Elder, my air group commander and mentor in the 1950s, who was in Class 4 at Patuxent. Elder retired as a captain, though he should have made four-star admiral. He was in command of an aircraft carrier when it bumped the bottom of San Francisco Bay, automatically ending his Navy career. He then joined Northrop and got involved in the highly classified Stealth program. Elder recently retired from Northrop, and he was replaced at the company by another TPS graduate, Paul Gillcrist. That shows how we stick together.

Thinking of Bob, I have to say we have reached the village "elder" age. Sorry, but that's the way my mind works.

I admit it—SETP is an exclusive society. I don't believe snobbery is involved at all, because professionalism is the criterion for acceptance. It has nothing to do with your ancestry or how you part your hair. We made a mistake, in my opinion, when we ruled that anyone who has flown at an altitude of fifty miles or higher is eligible for membership. Therefore, Walt Cunningham, who was on my Apollo 7 crew but is not a test pilot, is a member. This isn't intended as a dig at Walt. I just feel that society membership should be an emblem on a test pilot's sleeve. It should belong to him alone.

Many of the shuttle astronauts are test pilots and rightly belong. John Young, who had flown in Gemini and Apollo before commanding the first shuttle, is a fellow. Bob Crippen, Young's co-pilot on the first shuttle mission, is a member. And at our meeting in September 1987 we honored Gordon Fullerton, the first of the shuttle-only astronauts to become a fellow.

The society keeps tabs on its members, and I get real pleasure out of reading about my old buddies in our newsletter and yearbook. I see that Chuck Yeager is a fellow, as one would expect. And Jim Wood, who flew the X15 for NASA, is active in a civilian testing group at Mohave Air Force Base in California. Paul Thayer, a graduate of TPS 1, was the test pilot for Chance Vought in the 1950s who flew the first Cutlass. He is the guy we were going to see in Dallas when Duke Windsor ordered wheels up at 0900. Thayer became chairman of the board of LTV and then deputy defense secretary. He was convicted on an insider stock deal, but he has served his sentence and has since formed an electronics company. He's a brilliant manager and is making a comeback.

Bob Little, who excelled as a test pilot for McDonnell-Douglas, now has a corporate role in the company. Pete Conrad is also with McDonnell-Douglas, as a vice president. Jim McDivitt, who like Pete flew in Gemini and Apollo, is a senior executive of Rockwell International.

END OF A GENERATION

In the 1980s we are ending the first generation of military test piloting. Company flight tests were of course performed when aircraft were first manufactured, but the military program was not under way until World War II. The initial Navy class at Patuxent graduated in 1945. It was not TPS 1. The classes were designated by letters at first. My friend Tom Connolly was in the last of the lettered classes, Class OE—O for operation, E for the fifth of the series—which graduated in 1948. Class 1 also graduated in 1948.

I read the TPS Patuxent class rosters, and it's like a parade of friends passing in review. Bob Elder was the outstanding student in Class 4. Laurie Heyworth, a retired rear admiral who is married to Jo's stepsister, was the outstanding student in Class 5, and two of Laurie's classmates were Duke Windsor and Al Shepard. Bob Hoover was in Class 6, as was Bud Sickel, who cheered me on when I reached the 1,000-hour mark in jets. Don Shelton was in Class 7, Bob Baldwin was in Class 8, and on and on.

I'm not just reciting names for the sake of nostalgia. There's an important point I want to make. My world as a test pilot is the fighter world. You don't see bombers in my inventory. My image of a bomber cockpit is one of a bunch of guys milling around, smoking cigars and looking like Curtis LeMay, the commanding general of the Strategic Air Command (SAC), when I was a young Navy aviator. In a multi-engine aircraft there always seems to be room for somebody else. When a B-1 crashed in September 1987, there were six people aboard but only four ejection seats.

That's the way it was getting to be in the space shuttle before the tragic *Challenger* accident in January 1986. Before the shuttle—in Mercury, Gemini and Apollo—astronauts were aviators. Only Harrison Schmitt, a geologist, had no flying experience before joining the program, and he went through flight training while a space candidate. When Schmitt went to the moon on Apollo 17, he was a competent jet pilot.

The first shuttles were manned by test pilots—John Young, Bob Crippen, Joe Engle, Gordon Fullerton. But then NASA began putting others on board, people they called mission and payload specialists. Now I think of them as similar to members of a bomber crew—a bombardier, a navigator. The specialists have important duties to perform, but they should not be confused with pilots. Nor should people who don't fly the spacecraft be called astronauts.

We are in an area of critical distinctions. Take the case of *Voyager.* Dick Rutan, the pilot, is a test pilot and a member of SETP, as is his brother Burt. Jeana Yeager is a pilot, doubtless a good one, and she helped design and build the *Voyager.* But she is not a test pilot and is not a member of the society, though there are those who believe she ought to be. I say she's not qualified. We have a category of honorary fellow, and it has been reserved for such eminent aviation figures as Charles Lindbergh, Jimmy Doolittle and Jacqueline Cochran. Jeana Yeager would be in very good company as an honorary fellow.

SPEAKING OF ACCOLADES

Pilots of high-performance aircraft collect trophies like some people collect stamps. Many are not meaningful. Some are what I call ''show and tell'' awards, a plaque or a piece of crystal that comes with a ceremony and requires an acceptance speech. But others I regard as ultimate accolades. Being made a fellow of SETP is the highest honor accorded by my peers. Election to an aviation hall of fame is its equivalent in terms of public recognition.

I was inducted into the International Aviation Hall of Fame in San Diego while still an active astronaut in the 1960s. Then I was honored by New Jersey, my home state, and made a member of the Aviation Hall of Fame. It's located near my boyhood home, at Teterboro Airport, where I once hung over the fence and watched the idols of my youth. And there is one in New Mexico. It was founded at the urging of Jack Schmitt, who was elected to the U.S. Senate after leaving the space program.

Finally I should mention the National Aviation Hall of Fame in Dayton, Ohio, which is recognized by an act of Congress. Dayton is where military aviation had its beginning in 1907 with the establishment of the Aeronautical Division of the Army Signal Corps. I became a member in 1986, and two good friends were inducted in 1987—Tom Moorer, the retired admiral and former CNO, and Gus Grissom, posthumously. In addition to Bob Hoover, those to be honored in Dayton in 1988 are John Young and Pete Knight.

In 1963 the Mercury astronauts were the recipients of the Iven C. Kincheloe award. Kincheloe was an Air Force pilot who died while testing an F104, a supersonic fighter. The Kincheloe award, aside from being the highest honor bestowed by SETP, is a reminder of occupational risk. Test pilots are killed with regularity. In the early space program, too, there are seven names to remember—See, Bassett, Freeman, Williams, Chaffee, White, Grissom. As it says in the test pilot's creed, "Somebody has to give himself as the price of each frontier."

5 Mercury:
Get Ready, Get Set...

AND THEN THERE WERE SEVEN

I reported to the Pentagon on February 2, 1959, with no inkling why. I carried confidential orders that offered one clue—I was to dress in civilian clothes. Later I learned that President Eisenhower had insisted that the man-in-space program be a civilian endeavor. To join it, I would have to leave the Navy at least temporarily.

I found myself in an assembly hall with a few dozen guys like myself—a couple were Navy friends, test pilots—also dressed in civvies. Up on a stage were three gentlemen from the National Aeronautics and Space Administration, NASA.

On December 17, 1958, the fifty fifth anniversary of the Wright brothers' first flight, T. Keith Glennan, the administrator of NASA, had announced a manned satellite program. It was named Mercury for the son of Jupiter, who symbolized for the ancient Romans the safe return of man to earth. In January, 1959, NASA picked McDonnell Aircraft Corporation of St. Louis to build the spacecraft. In the contract, though, it was called a capsule, a mistake we'd have to live with for a while.

In February it was time to pick pilots. Despite President Eisenhower's reluctance to have the project identified with the armed forces, the wisdom of drawing from military test pilots was realized. A total of 508 service records were screened, and 110 were found to meet minimum standards—between twenty five and forty, no taller than five-eleven, a college degree, and so on. A selection committee had been named by Robert R. Gilruth, manager of the Space Task Group and boss of Project Mercury. The committee consisted of a senior engineer, a flight test engineer, two surgeons, two psychologists and two psychiatrists.

The 110 candidates—fifty-eight Air Force Pilots, forty-seven Navy aviators and five Marines—were divided into three groups and brought to Washington on successive weeks. By the luck of the draw I was in the first group. The third group was never summoned. Our enthusiasm, as NASA perceived it, was so great that seventy candidates were sufficient.

NASA's reasoning to cut the candidate total also led to a reduction in the number of openings—from twelve to six. NASA asssumed that few of us if any would drop out in training. That was valid, but the assessment of our early enthusiasm, at least in my case, was faulty. I showed interest because I was curious. In fact I was put off by the idea of flying in a capsule, a can without wings. I have a distinct impression of listening to the assurances of a NASA recruiter, whether or not I really did. "Not to fear," he said—if it was a dream, it was based on the kind of stuff they were telling us— "we'll fly chimpanzees first."

The three selection committee members who addressed us from the stage of the Pentagon hall were Charles J. Donlan, a senior engineer and Gilruth's assistant; Warren J. North, a NASA test pilot and engineer; and Lieutenant Robert B. Voas of the Navy, a psychologist. They must have looked into a sea of blank expressions. We were a very confused group of guys.

Only one of us knew the score, as I now understand. John Glenn was a Marine lieutenant colonel assigned to the Navy Bureau of Aeronautics in Washington. He had been a fighter pilot in World War II and in Korea—he too was on Air Force exchange in Korea, flying the F86. In 1957 he flew an F8U, the Chance Vought Crusader, from Los Angeles to New York at an average 723.52 m.p.h. It was a record—the first supersonic coast-to-coast flight. John big-dealed that flight, and I gave him credit for that. He did what I do with my flying feats—he made sure they were noticed.

Glenn then became a desk jockey in Washington, but that gave him access to the grapevine. He heard McDonnell was developing something, and when the first full-scale mockup of the Mercury capsule was rolled out for review at the St. Louis plant, he was there as an observer. He had decided to join the program before the rest of us knew about it, and he pulled strings. John was nudging the upper age limit—he would be forty in 1961—and lacked a required degree in engineering. But he was highly motivated, to say the least.

After a series of written tests and interviews the list was cut in March to thirty six eligibles, who were invited to undergo rigorous physical testing. I was one of them, and I decided to stay with it, my doubts notwithstanding. I had come very close to opting out. I wanted to fly the F4H, as I've said. I wanted to take "my plane" to the fleet as a squadron commander. I returned to Patuxent and sought the advice of men I respected, like Bob Elder and Don Shelton. They said that this was my chance to fly higher, farther, faster— and that's what all test pilots strive for. Go along with it, they urged. It might be fun to find out what's going on in the man-in-space program.

I would do the drill, but I kept my misgivings with me. I thought often about the ludicrous session at the Pentagon at which we were briefed by two NASA engineers and a Navy head shrinker. This was a great opportunity, we were told, to fly atop a rocket. I had little faith in rockets since nearly being killed while watching a Terrier test in China Lake in 1953. The Terrier, I was aware, was built by the Convair Division of General Dynamics, also the manufacturer of the Atlas, the rocket scheduled to send the Mercury spacecraft into orbit. In fairness to Convair the Atlas became a superb booster.

I would also come to enjoy piloting the spacecraft, but in early 1959 I was looking for the "no" desk, the place you go to say you want out.

I was the first or one of the first to call it a stunt, riding a wingless can into space on top of a rocket. I believed that the Space Task Group ought to be talking to trained athletes or circus performers, not test pilots. The idea of flying in something called a capsule bothered me for the length of the program. At first we joked about it. The astronauts coined the phrase "man in a can," not Chuck

59

Yeager or the guys out at Edwards, who according to Tom Wolfe in *The Right Stuff* changed it to "spam in a can." We argued strenuously for a change in terminologies. It wasn't until we were on our way to the moon, however, that we were flying a "spacecraft" launched by a booster. Even then the image persisted. Throughout the Gemini and Apollo programs the fellow on the radio at mission control in Houston was called Capcom, the capsule communicator.

Looking back from retirement, I'm able to joke about it. I was doing television commercials for Actifed, a cold remedy, and I was also making public appearances. "I used to fly in capsules," I would say. "Now I'm pitching them."

There were thirty two of us when we went for physical exams at the Lovelace clinic in Albuquerque, New Mexico. Officially called the Lovelace Foundation for Medical Research, it was a private facility under government contract, run by Randolph W. Lovelace, an expert in aerospace medicine. Lovelace would prove a point I often make about the death rate of doctors in airplane accidents. He was killed flying an Aero Commander in bad weather. I have lost a number of doctor friends who believe they can control their destiny because they make life-and-death decisions in a hospital.

I still feel that the physical exams at Lovelace were an embarrassment, a degrading experience. I have said many times—and meant it—that it was a case of sick doctors working on well patients. I make the point in talks to medical associations. It was a rare, almost unheard of situation in which so many healthy individuals submitted to an array of tortures—protoscopies, barium-enhanced X-rays, psychological interrogation and so on.

The doctors at Lovelace were trying to establish a physiological and psychological baseline to be used in tests during a space flight. That was a valid exercise, I would admit. It might even have amounted to justification for our agony except for one thing—it didn't work. According to Colonel William K. "Bill" Douglas, our family doctor in Mercury and our close friend, the punch-card computerized data obtained at the Lovelace clinic could not be interpreted. The tests had to be redone after those of us who were selected joined the program. Much as I'd rather not knock a dead man. Randy Lovelace did a lousy job.

The medical tests did turn up some minor problems. My throat was examined by an Air Force doctor, Brigadier General Al Schwictenberg. I still remember Schwictenberg clutching my tongue, making it impossible for me to inquire what was so interesting as he buzzed for another doctor. They peered intensely down my esophagus, and I feared it was serious. I was a heavy smoker then. As it turned out, the doctors had only discovered nodes on my vocal cords, the kind that had made the old movie actor, Andy Devine, famous for his gargle-sounding voice.

Only one candidate washed out at the Lovelace clinic—Jim Lovell, my classmate at test pilot school. He had a liver ailment. Happily, Lovell came back in the second round of astronaut selection with an upchit, a certification that he was cured. He would eventually make four spaceflights, two in Gemini and two in Apollo.

Pete Conrad was another who was not picked for Project Mercury. He was considered one smart ass-tronaut. I held the title until Conrad came along. There was no way I could compete with him. It was as if the medical testing method was designed for Pete to ridicule. His antics were hilarious.

Conrad is one of these people who manages a bowel movement about every third day, and the doctors made an issue over his inability to give a fecal sample. Finally he produced one the size of a coffee bean, and with some pride he brought it to the clinic in a one-pint plastic container. Plunking it on Schwictenberg's desk he said triumphantly, "This is for you, General." And it was Pete who suggested that we go to Old Town Albuquerque and eat a hot Mexican dinner on the night before we were to have barium enemas so they could X-ray our intestines. It was our only chance for revenge, he said with his gap-toothed, impish smile.

The thirty one of us who had passed at the Lovelace clinic reported to the Aeromedical Laboratory of the Wright Air Development Center in Dayton, Ohio, for physical endurance tests and psychological measurements. Bob Voas, who stayed with Mercury as our official head shrinker, explained we had been found fit. Now, he said, they were going to test our physical and psychological capabilities to respond effectively to the stresses associated with space missions.

I recall being placed in a dark and soundless room at the Wright center. It was so quiet I could hear my heartbeat. I found a pillow, put my head down on a desk, and went to sleep. I have no idea how long I was in that room or why I was there, nor did I care. We also took the Rorschach Test in Dayton—in which they flash cards with ink blots that are supposed to suggest images—maybe a butterfly or a Felix the Cat. When Conrad took the Rorschach and was shown a blank card, he baffled the doctors by insisting it was upside down.

Conrad was rejected for Mercury because, according to the doctors, his personality would not adapt to the isolation of a spaceflight. How wrong can you be? Pete flew the first long-term Gemini flight—he and Gordon Cooper were up for eight days, which then was a world record for manned spaceflight duration. As the commander of Apollo 12, he was the third man to set foot on the moon. And he spent a month in earth orbit when he commanded Skylab 2.

In mid-March, back at Patuxent, I got a phone call from Charlie Donlan, the unofficial chairman of the selection committee, who asked if I'd be willing to go to the Navy hospital in Bethesda for an operation on my vocal cords. I asked why, and he said there was just a small cause for concern. If I had the operation, he declared, and it was successful, I would be seriously considered for Project Mercury. After what I'd been through, I wasn't about to say no to minor surgery.

The doctor who did the operation was a commander, and I was a lieutenant commander. When he had me at his mercy—I was awake but under a local anesthetic and unable to speak—he said, "You must be someone damn important. I've never operated on a lieutenant commander. You must be going to the moon."

The selection was made in late March by Donlan, Stanley C. White, an Air Force doctor, and Warren North, the house astronaut or the equivalent of a company test pilot. To our great satisfaction, Donlan, White and North couldn't cut the eighteen finalists to six. Consequently, Bob Gilruth submitted seven names to NASA headquarters, and we were approved by the administrator, Keith Glennan. In mid-April our names were announced publicly.

Charlie Donlan had called me in a matter-of-fact way. He said, "We'd like to have you join us in Project Mercury, if you're interested." It was the NASA manner—always low key and studiously casual. I would come to question the approach when flight selections were being made, but for the time being I was faced with the most momentous decision of my life. This was my last chance to say, "Hell no. I'm not going to chuck my Navy career." But I had been conditioned by the winnowing process—the enthusiasm, the competition, my reaction to seeing others fall by the wayside. I decided to join, my misgivings aside.

TOGETHER AS A TEAM

We were seven veteran test pilots but unsophisticated young men in many ways, not very well prepared for the sudden fame of being America's first astronauts. We were small-town boys, by and large, coming from Sparta, Wisconsin, where Deke Slayton grew up on a farm, East Derry, New Hampshire, Al Shepard's home town, and Oradell, New Jersey, my boyhood home. And as military officers we had been isolated from the world.

Only John Glenn had known fame. After his record cross-country flight he appeared on a network TV quiz show, "Name that Tune." That's when he got interested in being a boy scout, a hero's hero, which he became. I've been told that he had been a typical Marine fighter pilot, boisterous and profane, but by the time I met him, he had changed.

We went to Washington in April 1959 for a press conference, which was a scary event, as we faced a thundering herd of reporters and photographers. Any gratification over the interest of the news media was tempered by an awareness that our private lives were in jeopardy. I still thank God for Walt Bonney, the chief NASA public information officer. He introduced us to Leo DeOrsey, a prominent Washington tax lawyer, who offered to become our agent and would not accept a fee. All we ever gave Leo were momentoes of our flights and some laughs. (Leo DeOrsey came to Cape Canaveral for one of our flights, and he inquired about a diet we used for bowel control, a low-residue diet. We answered in unison, "No shit, Leo.")

DeOrsey negotiated a contract with *Life* magazine for our personal stories, unofficial accounts of our experiences and those of our families. We were grateful for the money. I was earning about $12,000 a year then, and I regarded the contract as an insurance policy. Equally important, we'd be telling our stories to a few writers whom we could trust. The contract was criticized by the media and openly questioned by Kennedy administration officials. Eventually John Glenn presented our case directly to President Kennedy, whom he got to know after his Mercury flight in February 1962.

63

John explained in his low-key way that we had to cope with tremendous public interest in us and our families when we flew into space. Rather than having a slew of reporters banging down the door, we'd prefer to tell our stories to a select group. Otherwise we might not tell them at all.

It's true that during John's flight Annie Glenn refused to see Vice President Johnson but had allowed a *Life* writer to be in her house, though the scenes in the film of *The Right Stuff* of LBJ fuming on the street outside are fictional. The best explanation is that Annie felt comfortable with the *Life* writer, Loudon Wainwright, who had become a family friend.

We were officially assigned to NASA, on leave from our respective services. We retained our rank—I was promoted from lieutenant commander to commander during Mercury—but we were no allowed to wear our uniform except at funerals or on official visits to Washington. That disturbed me, as I am proud of being a naval officer.

A month before my Mercury flight, in September 1962, President Kennedy paid a visit to Cape Canaveral. I got a call from Walt Williams, the Project Mercury associate director, who said the president wanted to greet me at the launch pad. I knew there would be photos, and I sought permission to wear my uniform. When my request was turned down in Washington, I got my back up. I said they'd better keep those damn Air Force colonels far in the background. I was a naval officer, after all, and I didn't want it to look like I was a civilian working for the Air Force. The Air Force ran the missile range and used its authority to push us around, and I resented it.

A picture of my meeting with Kennedy hangs in my den. It shows several blue-suited officers crowding into lens range—all perfectly out of focus.

We were assigned to the Space Task Group headed by Bob Gilruth at Langley Air Force Base in Hampton, Virginia, just north of the entrance to the harbor at Norfolk. We each had a desk in one big office with a secretary, Nancy Lowe. It was a neat arrangement, as I look back, because it enhanced the kind of camaraderie that was so essential to our effort.

Right away, we started doing things as a group. I believe groups stimulate ingenuity, especially when they're composed of competitive people. We decided to quit smoking, for example, which was difficult for everyone but Gordo Cooper, the only non-smoker. Slayton and Grissom were typical Air Force cigar chompers, and Glenn, Shepard and Carpenter had all smoked. It was particularly tough for me. I had tried for years to break a pack-a-day habit, and each time I quit I became irritable and tense. Jo threatened to kick me out of the house.

Our smoke-ending scheme was far from foolproof. I smoked on and off for the next nine years. But it sure startled a few people. We had these small metal ashtrays, and we coated them with a thin film of gasoline. If a hot ash was flicked into an ash tray, it would ignite a flash fire. Fiendish but fun.

Our creative energies were not always put to such a beneficial purpose. As often as not our objective was to unsettle an unsuspecting person. It was at Langley that we initiated the gotcha series—"gotcha" as in "I've got you, sucker"—which would become space legend.

The first one was rather innocent. Stan White, an Air Force lieutenant colonel who was the chief flight surgeon of the space program, was the victim. White drove a new sports car, and he liked to brag about its efficient performance. So we plotted his comeuppance. For a week we added gasoline to his tank, a pint a day, and he raved about the great mileage he was getting. The following week we siphoned off a pint a day, and he went berserk. White never did figure it out.

My most beautiful memory of the Mercury program is how seven men—all superachievers with super egos—came together to work as a team. We had total faith in one another when it came to checking out a piece of equipment and reporting the results. So we were able to fan out across the country, each assigned a responsibility. Deke Slayton and Gordo Cooper monitored the boosters, for example—the Redstone, an Army missile built by Chrysler, and the Atlas by Convair. Al Shepard, who had been stationed at the Navy base in Norfolk and knew a number of black-shoe types, kept tabs on the recovery forces. John Glenn had cockpit layout, Gus Grissom had flight control, Scott Carpenter had communications and navigation, and I was in charge of life support systems, including the flight suit.

I'd go so far as to say that the most significant achievement of the space program was a concept of teamwork. A guy like Chuck Yeager is thus really out of place in my profession. I hesitate to snipe at Yeager, but he asks for it. He boasts about not being a team player.

When there was a problem to confront, we had subject-specific meetings. We called them séances as Tom Wolfe noted in his book, although the example he chose—John Glenn's objection to woman chasing—was unfortunate. One such séance had to do with a window. The spacecraft had been designed with portholes that appeared to us on the inside as shaped like a half-moon, and there was a periscope with a wide-angle lens that distorted the view. So we would be able to see the world or navigate by the stars. The eyeball was not being optimized, as we liked to say in engineering language. By this time we had made a commitment to going to the moon and back, which would require an ability to rendezvous and dock. How could we possibly rendezvous and dock without a window in the spacecraft?

We finally won. We got the window, but too late for Shepard's suborbital mission in May 1961. When he said there was a beautiful view, I don't know what the hell he was looking at.

We were also involved in the heat shield debate. For Shepard's flight beryllium was used to enable the spacecraft to withstand the heat of re-entry into the atmosphere. Of course, there was no re-entry on Al's flight, so the shield was only there for balance and ballast. On all later flights we used an ablative shield, which charred and cooked during re-entry. The point is we were consulted on engineering design down to the most minute detail.

We participated as well in planning our flights and in making complicated logistical arrangements, Harold Johnson, one of the STG engineers, came to our office one day with eight wrist watches— one for each of us and one he would wear. They were analog watches with numbered dials, but the numbers went from one to twenty-four. Six o'clock in the morning appeared as three to anyone who had used an everyday watch; noon was six, and midnight twelve. Johnson said we'd better become accustomed to these watches, because the worldwide tracking network was soon to go on twenty-four-hour time. They were confusing, to say the least. They were also unnecessary, since on our spacecraft clocks we would be reading digital time, as would the flight director and his crew in Mercury Control .

Two weeks later Johnson came by again, and we pounced on him. I led the attack. "What time is it, Harold?" He looked at the watch on his left wrist, the one with the twenty-four-hour dial, and hesitated. Then he tugged at his right sleeve and glanced at a watch with a standard dial. "Three P.M."

The seven of us, by the numbers, unstrapped the Johnson watches, as we called them, and placed them on our desks. We would not wear them, and that was that. There was no discussion, and Johnson beat a hasty retreat.

The worst experiences of our training phase were survival training exercises. They were grueling, for one thing, and they forced us to share with the program designers the uncertainty as to where a spaceflight might take us. We did jungle training in the wilds of Panama, we drifted in rafts in the Gulf of Mexico off the Florida coast, near Pensacola, and we were stranded in the Nevada desert, east of Reno.

By "stranded" I mean the seven of us were taken to a remote spot by military survival experts, taught the rudiments of a makeshift existence, and left to fend for ourselves. We had the rations we could carry in the capsule, and we had devices to use to assist in our rescue such as smoke bombs and flares. And of course we had the parachute with which we would have descended.

We were presumably alone on those survival exercises, though out in the desert we were joined by an unexpected intruder. He was Ralph Morse, an irrepressible photographer for *Life*. In fact Ralph was the principal photographer designated by *Life* to cover the astronauts. In the course of the association he became a close friend of all the astronauts and their families. Still, Morse was a journalist. When he was told by Lieutenant Colonel John "Shorty" Powers, an Air Force public affairs officer assigned to the astronauts, that survival training would be off limits, even for *Life*, Morse became determined to find us. He did, ingeniously.

Morse knew it was standard procedure in a desert survival exercise to display the parachute as a way of showing our location to search teams. So he chartered a small plane in Reno and flew around until he spotted the chute. No brilliance needed for that, but the next part is fun. Ralph had with him one-pound bags of white baking flour, which he used to mark the route. At each intersection on his way back to Reno he dropped a bag of flour. Then he simply rented a jeep and drove to our camp, following his flour markings. He arrived at our base camp on the evening before we were to deploy on individual exercises. We were stunned when he walked into camp and said, "Hiya fellas."

It was a good gotcha for Ralph, but he made the mistake of enjoying it so much that he was vulnerable to retaliation. While he was in our tent having a hamburger and a cookie, Shepard and I went out to his jeep and planted a smoke flare. We wired it to the engine block and strung a line from the actuator pull ring to the fan belt. Then we went back to the tent and said, "Ralph, your jeep is in the way. You'd better move it."

Ralph was still gloating and didn't suspect a thing. He got in the jeep and hit the starter. Blam! He was engulfed in a blanket of green smoke. He started to back up in an effort to escape, but it was no use. He was covered with green dust, and the jeep had to be towed back to Reno and sold for scrap. Ralph took it like a good sport, and of course we were delighted.

The desert survival course was memorable for serious reasons. In just two days we descended down the ladder of civilization and regressed to a primitive species of homo sapiens—Cro-Magnon comes to mind. It was so hot that we barely existed during the day and foraged for food at night. We had these special Randall knives, made by Bo Randall of Orlando, Florida, a friend of Cooper's, which were superior to what we'd been issued by the Navy and Air Force. We stored matches and fish hooks in the handles of the knives, held in place with candle wax. The wax melted and leaked out—it was that hot.

We were given just enough water to avoid dying of thirst—and not a drop for washing. John Glenn, the hard-nosed Marine, tried to save his water and nearly passed out. A certain amount of water is required to prevent dehydration in the desert. We learned that you drink the water you have until it's gone, and if you have not been found by then, you die of thirst. It doesn't help to ration your water supply.

In the early morning of the third day I was cooking boullion over a fire in a pan I had fashioned out of aluminum foil, and Cooper appeared. "Hey, Wally," he said. "They're saying we can leave now." I glanced at Gordo and thought he looked God-awful. I hoped I wouldn't get that bad when of course I already was, or worse. "Hey,

Wally," he repeated, "it's time to leave. They have food at the base camp." He started walking away.

"Where the hell are you going?" I demanded. They hadn't told us how long the exercise would last, and I guess I was half-crazed from the sun.

"It's over there, about a half-mile away. They've brought in breakfast."

"No," I said. "I want to eat my soup."

I finally did walk back to the base camp, and the Air Force had driven in a truckload of turkey and roast beef, salad and fruit. I grabbed a fresh peach, glistening and cold, ate it, and I was stuffed. None of us was able to eat more than an infant's portion. We were too dehydrated.

We went to Reno that night, to a hotel and casino called The Holiday. The proprietor, Newt Crumley, had become a friend. We were on liberty, so we gambled a bit and had fun. The next morning we went into the mountains to fish for golden trout, and a thought occured to me. Yesterday we were at the bottom of the human pile, I said to myself—dirty, unshaven, living in our underwear, groveling for a sip of water and a morsel of food. Today we are climbing to the peak of life's fulfillment.

We weren't the super athletes NASA might have hired for a stunt mission in space, but we were in good physical shape and getting better. We were serious about not smoking, though I didn't quit for good until 1968, when I flew in Apollo. We exercised by playing games like handball, and we skied and hunted and fished. Glenn was a serious jogger, running a regular two miles a day.

Physical conditioning was essential, because in space our bodies would undergo stresses the full extent of which was still a mystery to the aeromedical people. They tried to approximate the stresses, and built machines based on predictions—stress simulators. Some were useful training devices; others were merely instruments of torture.

One of those in the latter category was the Multiple Axis Space Test Inertial Facility, or MASTIF. It spun you up in all three axes at once—you were rolled, pitched and yawed—to a velocity of thirty r.p.m. The seven of us rode the stupid thing, and we all lost our cookies or nearly did. Our main objection to MASTIF was that it didn't simulate a situation that was likely to occur in space—a spacecraft out of control in all three axes. The only time there was an incident the least bit like it was on Gemini 8, flown by Neil Armstrong and Dave Scott. Armstrong and Scott came into the program with the second and third groups selected, in 1962 and 1963, and ironically they never trained on the MASTIF.

MASTIF was located at Lewis Research Center in Cleveland, and Al, Deke and I were there in the winter of 1959-60. It was snowing, windy and bitter cold. Nevertheless, Gus and Scott insisted on coming up. They were due to arrive by train on a Friday afternoon, since airplanes were grounded. I couldn't understand their determination to get to Cleveland on a Friday in the middle of winter until I realized they had a skiing weekend in mind. John and Gordo were on assignments elsewhere, or they would have joined us. We all enjoyed skiing, still do, and we liked doing things together.

In early 1960 we paid a visit to General Dynamics in San Diego, where the Convair Division manufactured the Atlas. It still did in 1988, as a matter of fact. As Atlas Centaur, now called an expendable launch vehicle, an ELV, our old booster is sending communications satellites into earth orbit for a consortium of European space agencies.

Scott Carpenter had lived in San Diego as a fleet aviator just before joining Mercury, and we were met at the airport by friends of Scott's who had two young sons in tow. The little boys asked for our autographs, and we complied of course. We were in San Diego for three or four days, getting to know the Convair crew, and it was then that Gus Grissom exhorted the plant employees to "do good work." When we departed, the same youngsters were at the airport, and they again asked for autographs. I asked what they had done with the ones we had given them, and I'll never forget the reply. "We traded them. They're worth two toads apiece."

Deke Slayton did not come to San Diego, and we would not learn why for a long time—not until just before he was supposed to fly, in 1962. Slayton had a medical problem that the doctors had discovered, but it would be kept a secret, even from the rest of us.

We had been doing centrifuge runs at a naval facility in Johnsville, Pennsylvania, officially called the Aviation Medical Acceleration Laboratory. The centrifuge could approximate the acceleration forces of a Mercury launch, ten G's or ten times our body weight. It is, therefore, a very rough ride. During the test we were strapped to a custom-fitted couch similar to one we would use in space, and we had sensors connected to our bodies for the purpose of recording

70

biomedical data. It was during these tests that Slayton's electrocardiogram, a graphic display of his heart function, indicated a fibrillation, an irregular heartbeat.

Bill Douglas, our personal physician, was one of the first to learn of the problem, and he made a strenuous but unsuccessful effort to restore Deke to flight status. Heart specialists were consulted, including Paul Dudley White, who had attended President Eisenhower when he suffered from coronary disease. I tell Deke today that he's alive while the doctors who grounded him are dead.

FOR ONCE AN ALSO-RAN

I joined the big boys when I joined the space program. I remembered my first year at the naval academy and how I learned that most of my fellow midshipmen had been captain of the high school football team or president of the senior class. I told myself then that not everyone can be number one, but in a competitive profession that's a reality not always remembered. As I was making a name for myself as a naval aviator, I forgot it completely. In my first year as an astronaut I was one of seven guys, a member of an elite team, and there was no pecking order. All of a sudden, in 1960, we were faced with flight selection. One of us was going to come out of the astronaut pack.

We worked for an agency of a bureaucracy—the Space Task Group was absorbed by the Manned Spacecraft Center, based in Houston— and it didn't take long for me to see how it differed from the Navy. We had watched with amazement as the associate director of STG, Charlie Donlan, was replaced by Walt Williams, who had run the X15 program. While we applauded the appointment of Williams, who had won the respect of test pilots, we saw his ascendency as a power play. Our eyes were opened to the possibility of a political factor in the success of a government official. The inevitable question was raised. Would politics be a factor in the manned space flight selection process?

The answer is yes, obviously. John Glenn was America personified—baseball, hot dogs and apple pie. From the standpoint of public relations he was ideal, as he demonstrated after he was the first to fly in orbit. I would hasten to point out, however, that politics was but one consideration, and John's primacy was the luck of the draw more than anything else.

Quite frankly, the way the flight selection in Mercury was handled by Bob Gilruth and company baffled and disturbed me. They played it close to the vest, so close that the media knew what was going on almost as soon as I did. In late 1960 Glenn, Grissom and Shepard were told that they were in the running for the first flight, a Mercury-Redstone suborbital mission. Cooper, Slayton, Carpenter and I were not told of the decision until it was about to be made public. *Life* came out with a cover photo and a story about the gold team, the three primary astronauts, and the four of us were devastated.

NASA wanted to perpetuate the myth of three coequal spacemen, but it was clear to us before long that Al Shepard would fly the first Redstone, then Grissom, then Glenn. John was furious when he learned he would be Al's backup, but that's a story I'd prefer not to get into. We are very close today, the seven of us, and I'd rather not open old wounds. There is no reason to. I have been critical of Chuck Yeager for degrading other people, seemingly to build himself up at their expense. I don't have any use for that.

John might have been unhappy, but he was still resourceful. He was soon saying that we really didn't need a third suborbital flight, and I found myself agreeing with him, as did Deke, Scott and Gordo. The four of us, it turned out, were playing into John's hands. We were sponsoring him for the first orbital. We were thinking in terms of first flight, second flight and so on. The distinction between orbital and suborbital was not all that clear to us. You can imagine my surprise when John became *the* first American in space, and the story got around that it had been planned that way from the beginning. That is just not the way it happened.

What did happen is that Gilruth called us into his office—it was on February 21, 1961, the day of a successful test of the Mercury-Atlas, MA 2—and announced the selection. Al would be the first to fly, then Gus, then John. We each shook Al's hand and complimented him, and that was that, although I wasn't the only one who remembered it as "them and us" day.

Right after we learned that Al would make the first flight, we went to Cape Canaveral for an unmanned test of the Mercury-Redstone. It was a memorable day, especially for someone who likes sick jokes. I was standing with Max Faget, the NASA engineer who had had the most to do with designing the spacecraft, as we counted down to launch. It got to zero and liftoff. "My God that was fast!" said

Faget, but when the smoke had blown away, we could see the Redstone still on the pad with the spacecraft in place.

We soon knew what had happened. The Redstone had shut down in the first second of flight and had settled back on the pad, but the rest of the events of the flight occurred on schedule. They included escape tower jettison, which is what we had witnessed. The escape tower is a rocket-powered device designed to carry the spacecraft away from the booster in a launch emergency. After launch the tower is separated from the spacecraft by the rocket and is destroyed. We watched the sequence unfold. It was all automatic, which is why we called the program the "chimp mode." There was a bloop, and out came the drogue parachute. Then another bloop—the main chute appeared, and it hung there like Mrs. Murphy's laundry. Finally a canister of dye exploded, and the air was full of yellow dust used to mark the spacecraft landing spot.

Humor was an essential ingredient of our existence at Cape Canaveral. It provided relief from very long hours of very serious preparation for flights into the unknown. More important, it palliated the frustrations of those early days in Mercury. We were lagging behind the Russians. On April 12, 1961, Major Yuri Gagarin of the Soviet Union made a single orbit of the earth in Vostok I, becoming the first human to fly in space. Shorty Powers got guffaws from around the world with his response to a press inquiry in the middle of the night. "We're all asleep down here," said Powers, who was to become known, whether he liked it or not, as "the voice of the astronauts."

Thank God for Bill Dana, who kept us laughing for years. His real name is Bill Szathmary, a professional comic who had an act about a frightened Mexican astronaut named Jose Jimenez. He would start off by saying, in his put-on accent, "My name Jose Jimenez," and in reply to a reporter's question about how he would occupy himself in space, he would answer, "I teenk I'm gonna cry a lot." But my favorite Dana line was this one: "Please don't say blastoff. We say liftoff. We take a blast before liftoff."

Dana was doing a one-night stand in Cocoa Beach near Cape Canaveral, and Al Shepard and I were in the audience. When Dana asked for a straight man, Al volunteered. Then I did, too. What we really liked about Dana is that he made himeself the butt of his jokes.

Like Bob Hope, also a dear friend of the astronauts, he did not get laughs at the expense of someone else.

On the launch pad for his flight, just before going up the elevator to the spacecraft, Shepard did a Jose Jimenez imitation, as Gus Grissom listened. "To fly in space you need four legs." said Al, accent and all. "Why is that?" asked straight man Grissom. "Because you need to be a dog."

It was Al's way of chiding the Soviets for sending canine crews, as if to mock the human element of space flight. We felt the same about chimpanzees. The flight of Ham, on January 31, 1961, was a source of some chagrin.

We resorted to jokes and pranks and good-natured kidding to relieve tension and boredom. As I often said, levity is the lubricant of a crisis. The uncertain reliability of the boosters and spacecraft caused many launch delays. When you get ready to go on a certain day, having put in long hours and knowing that your anxiety has been controlled by hard work, and then there is a scrub—the letdown can be agony. We set the record for delays with John Glenn's flight in February 1962. It got to the point where we were laughing at ourselves, but it wasn't all fun. We were showing our frustration.

Landwirth, the manager of the Holiday Inn in Cocoa Beach, had prepared a cake for the celebration of Glenn's success. It was a model of the Mercury spacecraft, built to scale. Landwirth had to rent a freezer truck to store it in, as we waited and waited. Landwirth is still a close friend. He is part of us. He comes to Mercury astronaut reunions, and he has been instrumental in a nonprofit scholarship program in behalf of space exploration, the Mercury Seven Foundation.

When Al Shepard was launched aboard *Freedom Seven* on May 5, 1961, I was flying a chase plane, an F106. Earlier in the program we had raised a fuss over the unavailability of aircraft, and Gordon Cooper—good old Gordo in his typical brash way—had leaked a story to the press. It worked. First we got a couple of F102s, which are marginally supersonic but satisfactory, and then we were upgraded to the F106, a Mach 2 fighter-interceptor. I had flown at Mach 2 in the F4H in 1958, so I was finally getting back to speed.

My plan on Shepard's launch was to follow the Redstone up, flying a spiral around it during early ascent. Right after liftoff, when the weight of the vehicle was just slightly less than the thrust of the booster, the Mercury-Redstone accelerated slowly, and I could literally fly rings around it. But of course as it burned off fuel, it picked up speed and would leave me behind. My purpose in the chase plane was to observe the booster and tell Shepard to abort, if there appeared to be a malfunction.

Anyway, I came up from Port Canaveral, heading north along the cape, but due to a brief launch delay I had to back off and circle around. All of a sudden they picked up the count, and I came burning up the cape, having used afterburner. I was able to stay with the Mercury-Redstone until about 30,000 feet, and all looked good. I say "good," not "A Okay"—that term was coined by Shorty Powers for public consumption. Scott Carpenter was in a second chase plane at 40,000 feet, but he could only watch as Shepard roared by.

As the blazing engine of the Redstone got smaller and smaller in the distance, I noticed that my air speed was dropping to zero. So much for Mach 2 in a prolonged vertical climb. I had nearly stalled out, but I quickly recovered from a momentary zero G experience.

Shepard's flight was a success. After five minutes and sixteen seconds of weightlessness he was recovered in the Atlantic. Gus Grissom flew an identical mission on July 21 aboard *Liberty Bell Seven*. It was not flawless. The hatch, held in place by explosive bolts, blew off shortly after landing in the ocean, and the spacecraft sank. Gus nearly drowned, as water filled his suit through the hole where the life support system had been connected. Gus was grateful to me, he said. A neck dam I had designed saved his life.

Gus had another reason to say thanks after I flew in October 1962. A question had persisted on the blowing of his hatch, and there were those who had maintained that Gus had inadvertently hit the plunger that exploded the bolts. When I was recovered, I remained in my spacecraft until being hoisted aboard the revovery ship. I then blew the hatch on purpose, and the recoil of the plunger injured my hand—it actually caused a cut through a glove that was reinforced by metal. Gus was one of those who flew out to the ship, and I showed him my hand. "How did you cut it," he asked. "I blew the hatch," I replied. Gus smiled, vindicated. It proved he hadn't blown the hatch with a hand, foot, knee or whatever, for he hadn't suffered even a minor bruise.

Our friendship had been solidified. Gus and I were next-door neighbors when we moved to Houston, and he asked me to be the executor of his will.

John Glenn flew his mission on February 20, 1962. He made three orbits and was in space for 4 hours, 48 minutes, 27 seconds. It was a momentous event for the United States. We were back in the game, which had been dominated by the Soviet Union. On May 25, 1961, twenty days after Shepard's flight, President Kennedy had delivered a special message to a joint session of congress. "I believe this nation should commit itself to achieving the goal, before this decade is out, of landing a man on the moon and returning him safely to the earth." John had gotten the lunar program off to a good start.

We had periods of anxiety during the flight of *Friendship Seven*, however. An attitude control thruster ceased to function on automatic, requiring Glenn to operate it manually. Ultimately he ran out of hydrogen peroxide fuel for both the automatic and manual control systems. And there was a disturbing humidity buildup in the cabin. To cope with it, Glenn had to adjust the flow of cool water into his suit, causing some discomfort due to overheating. Finally and potentially disastrous, we were getting a reading—it turned out to be faulty—that the heat shield was not locked in position. A decision was made to tell John to retain the package that contained the retrorockets once they had fired, slowing his velocity so he might re-enter the earth's atmosphere. The straps of the retropack, it was reasoned, might keep the heat shield in place, if in fact it had come loose. As the capsule communicator at Point Arguello in California, I was the one who passed the word on the third orbit. I advised John to retain the retropack until he was over Texas.

It worked out well. Glenn had reason to be concerned during re-entry, as he watched pieces of the retropack pass by his window, but he landed safely.

Deke Slayton was assigned the next flight—Mercury-Atlas 7, scheduled to fly in May, and I was Deke's backup. In late March I returned from a trip and went to pick up Jo at the Carpenters, who lived in quarters at Langley. It was a Friday night, and a party was in progress. Scott came out to greet me, and he wanted to talk. "Bad news," he said. "Deke's grounded." "You mean I have the flight?" I asked. "No," said Scott. "I have the flight."

That really hurt. Nothing against Scott, a neat, sweet guy. He was not my kind, though. Scott had been through test pilot school, but he was a multi-engine aviator and had been a communications officer on a carrier before joining Mercury. That's black-shoe to me. As the MA 7 backup, I believed, I was due to fly in Deke's place. So much for right and wrong. I felt the system was rotten. Here I was a fighter pilot standing aside for a bomber pilot. To make it worse, I was designated Scott's backup. I did my best and worked my tail off on Scott's mission. I don't think anyone knew how angry I was.

Those were not happy days. If I was at a low ebb, Deke was touching bottom. And our doctors, Bill Douglas and another surgeon named Bill Augerson, were bitter. They had tried to seek second, third and fourth opinions on Deke's heart condition from other doctors around the country, and all they got were wishy-washy answers. That's the trouble with a lot of doctors. They're afraid to commit themselves.

There was one positive result to Deke's grounding. The other six of us decided we'd ask him to be our leader, the chief astronaut. There had been rumors about NASA bringing someone in to oversee the astronaut office, and we feared it would be a retired admiral or general, possibly even Warren North, the "in-house" NASA astronaut, who definately wasn't one of us. What we wanted the least was somebody who would outrank us and issue orders in a military way. We wanted someone who knew us, who trained with us. Deke was the one and only choice. Sure, we were acting out of sympathy. Deke had been through hell. But we were proposing him as our leader out of respect not pity.

Gilruth okayed our proposal, and Deke Slayton was named chief astronaut.

Scott Carpenter's flight aboard *Aurora Seven* went reasonably well until it was time to begin the retrofire sequence over Hawaii. An attitude error of 25 degrees in yaw coupled with a three-second delay in the firing of the retrorockets caused the spacecraft to overshoot by about 250 miles. We knew we had a splashdown, but Scott was out of radio range, and we didn't know how he was doing. So the watching world was held in suspense for a few hours. NASA was criticized for withholding news of the landing, but that's the policy in aviation and in spaceflight. We don't say anything until we know the pilot's condition. We adhere to the policy out of consideration for the family.

Walter Cronkite, for one, got pretty emotional. He was in the CBS booth at Cape Canaveral for the three hours that Scott was out of touch in a life raft. Walter complained for months about NASA holding back information. I said finally, "Walter, you have to realize we can't tell you everything."

6

Mercury: ...Go for Six

In the long run I lucked out. Carpenter's flight was a rerun of Glenn's. I had been deprived of my turn, I belived, but I was ultimately glad of it. I was scheduled to fly Mercury-Atlas 8, MA 8, and I said I wanted six orbits. Gilruth and Williams refused to make a commitment. They were worried about the fuel supply. John and Scott had used up the hydrogen peroxide that powers the attitude control thrusters. My mission would be open-ended, but a recovery force would be deployed in the Pacific Ocean. If I did go six orbits, I would land about 275 miles northeast of Midway Island.

Earlier missions had been flown in the "chimp mode," the automatic mode, which wasted fuel. I argued that once a man was aboard it wasn't necessary to maintain the proper attitude for retrofire throughout the flight. The procedure had been to spin the spacecraft around right after separation from the booster—to get the heat shield pointed in the re-entry position and hold it there with the automatic program. I had a better idea and argued for it with Gilruth, Williams and James E. Webb, who had succeeded Glennan as the NASA administrator. "I can control attitude by hand," I said. "Let me shut

79

the spacecraft down and drift." I would start up again well before retrofire and return to retro attitude, using the manual controls.

I won my case. Once in orbit I walked the spacecraft around so slowly that I got only a glimpse of the Atlas. I fired my thrusters sparingly, in small bursts that I like to call micromouse farts. At the end of the flight I had over half of my fuel left and had to dump it. That was one of the ways I proved the purpose of putting a man in space, as opposed to a robot.

In Mercury we didn't have the capability of altering our orbit, as we would in Gemini and Apollo. But we could control our attitude axes of pitch, roll and yaw. Carpenter's flight had demonstrated the critical effect of attitude on a safe return to earth. I wanted to show how well I could operate the control system. I would shut down and start up and return to retro attitude by sighting on the horizon and the stars. We trained for that at a planetarium at the University of North Carolina in Chapel Hill.

On my flight I drifted for three orbits and then reacquired my attitude. We checked with the electronic program, and I was right on the money.

I proved man's advantage in space in other ways. With the photographic experiments, for example, I took the approach of an engineer rather than a sightseer. I sought advice from professional photographers such as Ralph Morse and Carl Mydans of *Life* and Dean Conger and Luis Marden of *National Geographic*. And I decided that a Hasselblad, with its larger film frame, was more suitable than a 35 millimeter camera. I had the Hasselblad adapted. A 100-exposure film container was installed, and an easy-aiming device was mounted on the side of the camera. Focusing would not be required from the infinity of space, I figured. Finally, I learned how to repair the Hasselblad.

Scientific observations were on my agenda as well. I observed the planet Mercury, not normally seen from earth, because the apparent position of Mercury is close to the sun. In orbit we're not affected by the diffuse light of the atmosphere, so I would see Mercury as it passed through layers of light. I tracked its passage against a yardstick of time.

I named my spacecraft *Sigma Seven*. Sigma, a Greek symbol for the sum of the elements of an equation, stands for engineering excellence. That was my goal—engineering excellence. I would not settle for less.

GOTCHAS AND GLITCHES

Someone I will forever remember fondly from space program days is Dee O'Hara, our nurse and also a babysitter to our kids. We allowed no one but Dee to draw our blood, not even the doctors, for fear that they would collapse a vein. She came to the crew quarters every morning as we prepared for a flight and was one of the last to see us off. A devout Catholic, Dee counted beads when we went on missions.

As good a friend as she was, Dee was still a gotcha victim. In fact, the better the friend the better the chance of being victimized. Gordon Cooper was my backup for MA 8, which meant he was with me in the final days of preparation, living in isolated quarters in a building on Cape Canaveral known as Hangar S. Dee collected our urine samples each day, so we decided to prepare the ultimate urine sample. Early one morning we filled a five-gallon bottle with warm water, figuring it would cool to body temperature by the time she arrived. We added a bit of iodine to give it color, laundry soap to make it foamy, and put the bottle on Dee's desk. I tagged the bottle, writing the time of delivery in Greenwich Mean Time, and I attached a bunch of lollipops. Gordo and I were like little kids, peeking with glee around the corner of the doorway, when we spotted Dee first stop in horror and then burst out laughing.

As I understand it, the first game of gotcha was played on a golf course. A pro had been challenged by a duffer. "How can you possibly compete with me?" asked the pro. "Well," said the duffer, "I'd like a slight advantage. I'd like to have two gotchas." "Fair enough," said the pro. "Is that like two strokes?" "Very much the same," said the duffer. On the eighth green the pro, who was comfortably ahead, bent to putt. Suddenly the duffer took his putter and goosed the pro, who hit the ball clear off the green and blew the hole. "That," said the duffer, "is my first gotcha," and he went on to win the match.

Obviously, the key to the gotcha game is expectation, and Dee O'Hara played very well. A piece of equipment we wore in those days without comfort facilities in space was a yellow plastic bag, otherwise known as a policeman's friend. I dressed for my flight

81

in a special room with the help of technician Joe Schmitt. Dee was not there, but she had laid everything out. I looked, and to my dismay I saw this big black rubber thing. It was a urine bag that would fit a horse, about ten times the regular size. I put on a bathrobe and walked to Dee's office with this bag flopping between my legs, and she went into mock shock. "Exactly the right fit," she said.

The Atlas is a volatile missile. It looks like a stainless steel sausage. The steel is very thin so as to reduce weight. To maintain rigidity, the Atlas is pressurized by its fuel, a combination of kerosene, liquid oxygen and gases. When there is an Atlas mishap, it's spectacular.

As I prepared for my flight, I was disturbed that the Atlas was blowing up regularly. This was the military Atlas, an ICBM launched in a series of tests at Vandenberg Air Force Base in California. It had not been man-rated, meaning checked over minutely for the sake of a man's life. As we had said on the visit to the Convair plant in San Diego in 1960, we didn't want the military Atlas, we wanted our own special bird. Nevertheless, in the summer of 1960 at Cape Canaveral, we had watched a Mercury Atlas go out of control and blow up during launch.

The Air Force grounded the Atlas, the weapons system, shortly before my flight in October 1962, which was one way of quieting reports about it blowing up.

There was another problem, and it nearly caused a delay. In July the Atomic Energy Commission had conducted a high-atmosphere nuclear test over the Pacific, creating a new zone of radiation, lower than the Van Allen Belts. By the end of August the hazard seemed negligible, but dosimeters were attached to my spacecraft and to my suit, and I carried three of them, so I could take real-time radiation readings. One read from 0 to 1 rad, which is a very small amount. A second read from 0 to 10, and a third read from 0 to 100. I didn't get a reading on any of them, which was a surprise. We reasoned that I was well protected by the insulation of the spacecraft.

With launch day approaching we had two major concerns: worldwide weather conditions, especially in the prime recovery area in the Pacific; and "glitches" on the MA 8 vehicle. Some component would check out okay one day but not the next for no apparent reason. We called this sort of perplexity a glitch, a term that originated in the electronic world. A glitch is a phenomenon that is not repeated and often cannot be explained. It causes a light bulb to go out for a second, or it is a change in the amplitude of a power supply that causes a computer to dump. Fortunately there were few of them, as we got ready to begin the count.

COUNTDOWN AT THE CAPE

The day began at 1:40 A.M. when I was awakened by Howie Minners, an Air Force surgeon assigned to Mercury. I showered, shaved and talked with Gordo Cooper, who was leaving for the launch pad to monitor spacecraft preparations. I then had the ritual breakfast of steak and eggs with Bob Gilruth, Walt Williams, Deke Slayton and Dr. Minners. We also ate a bluefish I had caught. That's a story I can finally tell, since the statute of limitations has expired.

Cape Canaveral is a strip of sand that juts north from the Florida mainland along the Atlantic Ocean. For centuries it was barren, only rattlesnakes thriving in the palmetto bushes. No signs exist of a sugar plantation implied by its Spanish name. When the missile range was established in the 1950s, the rattlesnakes were driven off—many wiped out by exploding rockets, according to local legend. By 1962 the Cape had become a recreation area for government employees. It offered excellent surf fishing, especially in the spring and fall when bluefish are running.

On the evening before launch Slayton and I went fishing. We hooked several bluefish in the five-pound range, but they fought free by severing our leaders with their razor-sharp teeth. I managed to land one by slinging it on the beach and pouncing on it before it could wriggle back to the surf.

The Cape is lined with missile gantries, and Deke and I had paid little attention to which was which. We were vaguely aware that a Thor-Delta stood about a hundred yards away, since it's a big vehicle, about the size of a Mercury-Atlas, and a military satellite booster. But we were so intent on catching fish that we were oblivious to activity at the pad. It wasn't until we heard a roar that we realized the Thor-Delta was lifting off. We were looking right up the tailpipe of its monster engine, and we knew right away that we were in the danger zone. Had there been an abort, it would have been a bad day for Mercury, with the chief astronaut and the pilot of MA 8 incinerated like the legendary rattlesnakes.

Anyway, the bluefish was delicious that morning.

I was relaxed at breakfast. Gilruth and Williams looked nervous, so I asked, "You guys worried about something?" That took the edge off. Walt Bonney, the PR chief from headquarters, had asked what newspaper I wanted to read on the morning of my flight. The *New York Times,* I said, having grown up in nearby New Jersey, and I thought no more about it. Sure enough, Bonney walked in that day with a copy of the *Times* dated October 3, 1962. I knew it was authentic, for there was a story on the front page about my mission that day. I realized the paper had been flown from New York, at no small expense. I was so impressed that I kept the copy.

Howie Minners escorted me to the pad. We rode in the transfer van, so called, though it was just a truck, a tractor-trailer. I was suited up with the visor of my helmet closed, so I would breathe pure oxygen and purge the nitrogen from my system. Minners was yakking away to keep my spirits up, which wasn't necessary. I wanted to rest and think about my flight. I could have unplugged my radio, but that would have been rude, so I signaled that I wanted him to stop talking by closing my eyes. Next thing I knew Minners was tapping my visor and saying by radio, "Wally, we're at the pad." I had dozed off.

Cooper did me one better when he flew the MA 9 mission seven months later. Gordo actually fell asleep on the launch pad when there was a delay in the countdown. The point was made repeatedly throughout the space program. The crew was always more relaxed than anyone else. It's a tribute to our training, and it shows the confidence we had in the people who supported us, both from NASA and the contractors. We could ask questions of technicians at the pad, or construction guys, and get straight answers. And we could call the executives, like Mr. Mac of McDonnell, and they too would level with us. That's one reason we completed Mercury with seven healthy astronauts.

We had anxious moments, sure. The pilots might have been cool, but everyone else experienced tension. When Cooper flew on May 15, 1963, I was Capcom, the capsule communicator in Mercury Control at the cape. Launch time neared, and my palms were damp. It's called the sweaty hand syndrome.

B. G. MacNabb of Convair greeted me at Pad 14 and wished me a happy landing. I took the elevator to the spacecraft, and Cooper was there, literally looking over the shoulder of Guenter Wendt, a German-born McDonnell employee, called the pad leader. Behind his back I referred to him as the "pad fuehrer," but I had come to admire his authoritarian manner. I also knew that Wendt was responsible for the spotless condition of the spacecraft. I did a white-glove inspection and didn't find a single spec of dust.

At 4:41 A.M. I was aboard *Sigma Seven*.

The count moved right along. There wasn't a lot of time to think, except about Jo and our two children—Walter M. Schirra III, known as Marty, the family middle name, and Suzanne, whom we called Suzy. Marty was twelve and Suzy five. My family was in Texas watching on television. Rene Carpenter had come to Cape Canaveral to watch Scott's launch, but she was the exception. More typically, our wives stayed home and watched the launch with the other astronauts' wives. The women were close to one another. Their group loyalty was such that they could usually relieve any discord that developed among the seven guys.

It occurred to me before launch that I had never slept in our new house. When I came to the Cape in August to prepare for my flight, we were living near Langley Air Force Base. But the Space Task Group, now named the Manned Spacecraft Center, was moving to a site on Clear Lake south of Houston. We had built a home near the new headquarters, and the family moved into it in September. I had said good-bye to them in Virginia and would come home to Texas, hopefully having made six quick trips around the world.

Of course I thought about how I'd handle the mission. I had made the point to NASA that my interest in public relations was zero. Nor did I intend to extol the wonders of space or portray the spectacle in vivid language. I was a pilot, an engineer, maybe a scientist. Sightseeing was low on my list of priorities. If it was poetry they expected, they should have sent a poet.

ON UP TO ORBIT

We had a near-perfect count with only a brief delay due to a radar malfunction at the tracking station in the Canary Islands. Liftoff was at 7:15. At ten seconds into the flight there was a problem I didn't know about then, but it came close to ending my fun. The clockwise roll rate of the Atlas was greater than planned, and it startled people in Mercury Control who were reading the instruments. My course was being plotted against an overlay grid called a harp, since it's shaped like the musical instrument. Green lines in the middle of the grid designate the safe zone, and on the outer limits the lines go from yellow to red. I was headed into the yellow area. If I had reached the red, there was a likelihood that the Atlas would impact on land, possibly in a populated area. In that situation the range safety officer would have had no choice but to abort the mission.

He would have pushed a button to destroy the booster, and I would have had to depend on the escape tower. The tower would automatically pull the spacecraft away prior to the destruction of the booster, and I would have been carried by parachute to a landing in the Atlantic. I was fortunate. The program straightened itself out, and the Atlas stayed within safe limits. We were on course. I didn't learn of the close call until after the flight.

None of us ever did use the escape system in Mercury—or in Gemini and Apollo. It was not an exercise we cared to practice. All we know is that it would have been a rough ride with a high probability of injury.

Once in orbit at an altitude of 176 miles, I began my turnaround with my attitude control system in the fly-by-wire mode. It's called semi-automatic, because the thrusters are fired electronically. But I controlled the firing. I was flying the spacecraft. With my eyes fixed on the control panel, studiously ignoring the view, I began a slow—four degrees per second—cartwheel. Once in the correct orbital position, I checked my fuel. I had used less than half a pound of hydrogen peroxide. The thruster jets worked perfectly. They responded crisply to my touch and shut off without any residual motion. I was able to make tiny single pulse spurts, the micromouse farts, to assume an exact attitude position.

I also was able to track my spent sustainer engine, as it followed in the distance. I concluded that a rendezvous of vehicles in space was feasible, given sufficient maneuvering thrust and precise attitude data.

Over the Canary Islands I tried the manual-proportional control mode, a mechanical system, and I found it sloppy. It tended to overshoot. Over Africa I switched on the automatic stabilization and control system, the auto-pilot.

Glenn and Carpenter had experienced suit overheating, and I was feeling it too. It was serious. Chuck Berry, our chief flight surgeon,

and Frank Samonski, our environmental supervisor, discussed bringing me back after one orbit. But on Berry's advice Chris Kraft, the
flight director, gave an okay for a second orbit, which was relayed
to me by Scott Carpenter in the tracking station at Guaymas, Mexico.

The suit had been my special area of responsibility, and before
the flight I had devised a procedure if overheating occurred. I
inserted cool water into the system at a very slow rate, advancing
the knob a half a mark at a time and then waiting ten minutes. My
logic was that if I added water in a hurry, a heat exchanger might
freeze, and then I'd be in real trouble. As I was nearing the end of
the first orbit, the temperature needle started to drop. It had reached
ninety-plus degrees, which was hot but not unbearable. The problem
was solved through no great amount of human ingenuity, but the
point was it was solved by a human. Later I received a plaque which
read: "Presented by the undersigned, who sweated more than you
did during the first orbit of MA 8..." The undersigned were Samonski
and his crew, the environmental controllers, and the valve I used
to control the water flow was mounted on the plaque.

As I worked with the cooling system, I discovered the source of
the mysterious fireflies that John Glenn had observed outside his
spacecraft. Water vented from the heat exchanger went overboard
in the form of water vapor—not steam but molecular water. When
it froze in the coldness of space, it crystallized, forming floating
particles. The phenomenon was reported by both Glenn and Carpenter. Scott called them frostflies. John saw them as fireflies,
because of the prism effect when the sun hits them, creating a color
display.

"I have a delightful report for one John Glenn," I said as I
approached California on the second pass. "I do see fireflies."

I had performed reference checks for the yaw attitude of the
spacecraft, its left and right orientation, and they had proven satisfactory. According to the flight plan I was to phase into drifting flight
during the third orbit. I gave a systems status report to Slayton and
I proceeded to cage the gyros, meaning to orient the gyroscopes
to a precise attitude—and to cut off electrical power . During the
drift I did a psychomotor experiment. I closed my eyes and tried
to touch certain dials on the control panel. I missed only three out
of nine, concluding that my sense of direction and distance had not
been impaired by weightlessness.

THE GOOD WORD FROM GUS

I powered up the spacecraft over the Indian Ocean and switched to fly-by-wire to check out the systems. I had sighted the moon through the window, and I reported to the station in Muchea, Australia, that I had fixed my attitude using the moon as a reference point. I then locked the system in automatic. I knew the ground stations had been paying close attention to my fuel usage, as Mercury Control was deciding how long I'd stay up. I got the word from Gus Grissom at Kauai, Hawaii. "Wally, you have a go for six orbits." "Hallelujah," I replied. I was to become the American who had flown the farthest in space.

I radioed Glenn at Point Arguello, California, that I was about to begin drifting again, and for an hour or so I observed the earth and took photographs.

Al Shepard was aboard ship in the Pacific, a tracking ship and not part of the recovery force, and I radioed to him a status report on the fifth orbit. My fuel supply stood at 81 and 80 percent in the automatic and manual tanks respectively. My oxygen was at optimum pressure. My suit temperature was a comfortable sixty two degrees. "I could say that you were definitely go," said Al.

Grissom in Hawaii read me a correct time for the retrofire sequence on the next orbit, and I heard Carpenter in Mexico and Glenn in California confirm that communications ought to be in good shape for re-entry. I was then astonished to hear a voice interrupt from Quito, Ecuador. We had what we called a minitrack there, a miniature tracking station, and it wasn't supposed to come on the air except in an emergency.

"Sigma Seven," he said, whoever he was. "Do you have a message for the people of South America?" I was furious. Here I was preparing for the crucial re-entry, and I was expected to utter some hogwash, some glowing statement about how I was proud to be an emissary of the United States, passing over Ecuador. "Roger, Quito," I radioed. "Buenos dias, you-all." And I was gone.

I knew I would be critcized for being brusque, and sure enough the telegrams, most of them protests to NASA, were handed to me on the recovery ship. But there was one I treasured from a U. S. diplomat in Ecuador. He said in effect that Schirra had proved his devotion to the people of Latin America by wishing them a good day. And by addressing them as "you-all," Schirra was simply noting that he was soon to become a resident of Texas.

SPOT-ON LANDING

It was time to get ready for the retrofire sequence. I switched to the fly-by-wire control mode while over Africa, and as I came up on the Pacific tracking ship, I positioned the spacecraft using celestial reference points. I reported my fuel supply to Shepard—78 per cent in both the automatic and manual tanks. Then I switched to the automatic control mode and was satisfied that its high-energy thrusters were working well. I had the manual-proportional system as a back-up. I was feeling fine, I assured Al.

The flight plan called for me to position the spacecraft using manual controls, then switch to automatic for retrofire, because the power of the big thrusters offsets the unbalancing force of the retrorockets. The retrorockets exert their force through the center of the spacecraft, so they don't kick it off course. That's what the book says, although it's not totally true. The high thrusters of the automatic system are designed to offset any perturbations resulting from retrofire.

Of course we trained for many hours in a simulator to control retrofire manually. It's good we did, because Gordon Cooper got a chance to fly by hand during retrofire when he flew in May 1963. In the course of twenty-two orbits the electronic systems failed, and Gordo had no choice but to manually guide the spacecraft.

In the simulator we had a regular spacecraft control stick. We designed the stick, incidentally—that's the engineering part of being a test pilot. You push it forward and back to control pitch, right and left for roll, and for the yaw motion you twist the hand grip just like on a motorcycle. The retrorocket offset could be introduced by a simulator technician, and we would either manage them or be taken on a wild ride. Bob Rushworth, an experienced X15 pilot, tried the simulator, as I observed him and tried to guide him. He had a hell of a time.

I armed the rockets on Shepard's command. Then I punched a button to initiate the sequence—the first, the second, the third... The retros fired with crisp precision, and *Sigma Seven* was holding steady as a rock. I switched back to fly-by-wire for re-entry, again according to plan. When I jettisoned the retro pack, I felt the spacecraft wobble and made a quick adjustment. I pitched up to a fourteen degree re-entry attitude and used the automatic controls to damp out motion. Then I switched on the RSCS, the rate stabilizing control system, as had been requested by the engineers. The RSCS is a fuel guzzler, but I had plenty. The gauge for the automatic system was reading between 52 and 53 percent. I allowed as how I was thrilled, in case anyone was able to listen through the ion or communications blackout.

At 40,000 feet I punched a button and felt the drogue parachute pop open. I activated the main chute at 15,000 and watched it blossom at 10,500. "That sort of put the cap on the whole thing," I said. I was elated, and I radioed Shepard, "I think they're going to put me on number-three elevator." I was of course referring to an elevator on *Kearsarge,* the recovery carrier. Actually I missed the carrier by only four and a half miles. The crew saw my contrail and heard sonic booms. Then my parachute came into view—truly a beautiful sight. If the chute hadn't appeared, of course, the day would have been a bust.

I had joked about *Sigma Seven* being a neat spacecraft and a lousy boat, but I decided to stay aboard her. I had had a bad experience in ocean survival training, being lifted from a life raft to a helicopter. I had bonked my head and almost fallen out of the sling. I preferred to be towed to the carrier and hoisted aboard. Within minutes a whaleboat was alongside, and the underwater team had the flotation collar in place. When I stepped from *Sigma Seven* to the deck of *Kearsarge*, it was ten hours from launch, almost to the second.

When I reached the admiral's quarters, where I would live during three days of medical tests and debriefings enroute to Hawaii, I found a memento from Dee O'Hara, the nurse. Hanging in the head was an oversized urine collection device, a duplicate of the one she had presented to me before the flight. Dee had given it to one of the doctors to bring all the way from Cape Canaveral.

There was a big greeting when we landed at Pearl Harbor, and I stayed in Hawaii for a day, lodged in Air Force VIP quarters. I was surrounded by dignitaries—the governor, a U.S. senator and military brass. Bill Dana happened to be in Hawaii. He telephoned and got through, with some difficulty.

"Hi Wally, how are you?"

"Oh, I've been around." Then clunk, I hung up. It was too good to resist—one of my better puns at the expense of a big-name comedian.

It was Houston's first chance to welcome a returning astronaut, and even though we arrived at about one in the morning, the governor was at the airport, the mayor, and other politicians from Washington and Texas, NASA officials and a whole lot of everyday people. Jo and all the astronauts and their wives met me too, and we had quite a celebration followed by a motorcade to our new home in Timber Cove, south of Houston. Then we drank champagne, and it was close to four in the morning before everyone left.

I was in my pajamas and ready to go to bed when Jo said, "Wally, will you please put out the garbage." What I had done to Bill Dana in Hawaii was nothing to what my wife had just done to me. The ultimate put-down.

Are You A Turtle, Wally?

At three minutes into my flight, when we were still in the Atlas boost phase, Deke Slayton came on the radio with a question I didn't quite expect. "Hey, Wally, are you a turtle?" Of course I knew the answer, but we were on live radio, and I wasn't ready for all the world to hear it. So I switched my mike to voice record, uttered my reply, clicked back, and said to Deke, "Rog."

Pilots have been asking each other the turtle question in barrooms since World War II, and if you don't give the right answer, you must buy a drink of the questioner's choice. The turtle society is based on ambiguous meaning, double entendre. An ass is not part of the human anatomy but a four-legged animal. What can a man do standing up, a woman sitting down, and a dog on three legs? The answer is shake hands. Or what is a four-letter word ending in K that means "intercourse"? The answer is talk.

Once aboard *Kearsarge*, when I had a little time to myself, I asked the communications people for a copy of the first few minutes of radio transmissions on flight, and they produced it. I had my tape recorder set in anticipation of a reunion aboard the ship. Deke and the other astronauts, along with Walt Williams, were on their way out via Midway Island.

We hadn't been together more than ten minutes. We were there in the admiral's quarters—all but Al Shepard, who was stuck in Japan, where the Pacific tracking ship had docked. The guys were all congratulating me. It was Walt Williams, in his fast-chatter way of talking, who demanded to know what my answer to Deke had been.

91

I flipped on the recorder, and there it was. "Wally, are you a turtle?"
"You bet your sweet ass I am."

BEYOND MERCURY

Jo, Marty, Suzy and I went to Washington on October 16. President
Kennedy was preoccupied with the Cuban missile crisis, but he had
time for a private ceremony in the Oval Office. He was kind to the
children, asking Suzy her age. She held up five fingers, as young
kids do, and he took her to see his daughter Caroline's pony,
Macaroni.

The astronauts were back in Washington after Cooper's flight in
May 1963. Over a series of White House visits we had traded friendly
taunts with the president. Kennedy had fumbled a medal when he
was awarding it to Shepard—we all received distinguished service
medals. As he was making the presentation to Glenn, Al whispered
in his ear, "Don't drop it." This time it was JFK's turn, and I was
the one he nailed. "By the way, Wally, are you a turtle?" I had to
think twice before saying, "You bet your sweet ass..." to the president of the United States.

President Kennedy also said to me, "I understand you have no
political aspirations." He had heard that from his brother Robert
Kennedy, the attorney general. Robert Kennedy helped initiate John
Glenn's career in the Senate. During my postflight White House visit
he took me aside, congratulated me and then asked, "By the way,
we are quite curious about your political ambitions." "I'm an
engineering test pilot," I replied. "And I'm becoming something
of a scientist. That is to say that my decisions are based on facts,
and I would find the transition to politics impossible." He then
escorted me to the Oval Office, and that was that. He may have
believed he had paid me a compliment, but I didn't see it that way.

When I got back to Houston, I wrote a post-mortem review of
my mission, a point-by-point critique. I'd stored in my head a number
of gripes about training procedures and how the flight was conducted, and I let fly.

I said there had been too much emphasis on the number of hours
per training effort and not enough emphasis on training results.
Performance shouldn't be evaluated, I argued, by numbers. It should
be evaluated by responses to various situations. There had been a
similar problem with spacecraft tests before reaching the launch
pad. Astronaut participation in certain areas of these tests, I

recommended, should be canceled. I have never been impressed by total pilot hours, and I used a favorite analogy. A transport pilot can log as many as ten hours in a flight, while a fighter pilot rarely logs more than two hours. Yet the fighter pilot's job entails a takeoff and a landing and some critical moments in between.

I repeated an argument we had been making for three years. I said there had not been sufficient emphasis on our maintaining proficiency in high-performance aircraft. Too much time had been allotted to "bull-session meetings" instead. I also raised the issue of physical conditioning. I'm not a fan of in-the-bedroom calisthenics, preferring competitive outdoor sports.

I also commented that in the last two weeks of mission preparation there had been an influx of personnel who needed to be educated about how the flight was going and who seemed to feel they must investigate all areas. The crew was therefore involved in all sorts of presentations when we could not afford the time. There was also interference from people who wanted information from me about the flight, when they might have provided me with helpful details. One such detail was a final version of the flight plan. It had been rewritten in Houston without checking with me. Consequently the printed flight plan in the form I'd intended to use it was not available until very late in the program.

I had a final complaint about the preflight period. For some reason people don't believe we have personal problems like everyone else. We need time to take care of the bank account, to review insurance policies and a will, and to attend to legal matters. In addition to the normal personal concerns I was moving my family at the time of my flight. Unlike military commands in which I'd served, NASA didn't provide the necessary assistance, not even a legal officer.

I then talked about the shaky decisions forwarded to the flight director about the suit circuit control during my flight. This was a critical problem. Information was available to Mercury Control Center about the status of the suit inlet temperature and the cabin dome temperature, both of which were consistent. This information was available prior to Guaymas, and there should have been no concern whatsoever about a GO decision for another orbit, yet there was. The flight controllers obviously still did not believe that I had valuable and valid information. Looking at the data used in Mercury Control Center, I understood the concern. Looking at the data that I made available, there should have been no concern. This was intolerable lack of faith in a test pilot's performance.

I said that as a test pilot I had successfully achieved, in my judgment, a rapport with engineers. So it was time that engineers were trained in maintaining rapport with the test pilots. The absence of faith in pilot control of the suit circuit was an example of lack of rapport.

Finally, I commented on communications control. That it had failed was in part due to improved communications capabilities. Many stations could transmit to me, while I was not transmitting to them. It was also apparent that Mercury Control Center had a very poor communications system. My recommendation for communications control was simple: "Don't call me. I'll call you."

MERCURY POSTSCRIPT

As *Sigma Seven* lifted off, there were nine very interested observers at Cape Canaveral. They were the nine new astronauts who had just reported for duty, the Gemini astronauts, as they would be called. I was too busy to pay much attention to them before my flight, but among my memorabilia is a picture of them watching me go. It shows Pete Conrad with his fingers crossed. Two of the nine, Conrad and Jim Lovell, were old friends from test pilot school. The rest would be good buddies too. We became an integrated team, as the lines dividing the old boys and new boys disappeared.

The next step to the moon was Project Gemini, named for Castor and Pollux, the twin sons of Jupiter. Twins were appropriate, for the larger spacecraft would carry two men. We would fly for periods of up to two weeks. We would perform EVAs, extra-vehicular activities or spacewalks. And we would maneuver in space, enabling us to rendezvous and dock with other vehicles.

Deke Slayton was still grounded and serving as chief astronaut. John Glenn, Al Shepard and Scott Carpenter also were taken off flight status due to disabilities. Grissom, Cooper and I flew in Gemini. In fact Gus was concentrating his effort on Gemini even while Cooper and I were flying in Mercury. He was angry about being blamed for his spacecraft having sunk, and he was fighting to come back out of the pack. Gus was a tiger. He wanted the first Gemini flight, and by God he got it.

I went back to Cape Canaveral to get my car, my boat and trailer, and other belongings. I also brought the big black bag back to Dee O'Hara. I was ready to leave, but there was an Atlas launch, and I stayed to watch it. I went out to Hangar S and up an iron-rung ladder to the roof, where there is a viewing platform. It's about four miles from the pad.

We listened to the count on a radio speaker, three, two, one, liftoff. At about 100 feet off the ground the missile was destroyed. There were pieces of the Atlas all over the horizon. I was thinking, oh my God!

My father was a barnstorming stunt pilot. He stands here with his
DeHaviland biplane.

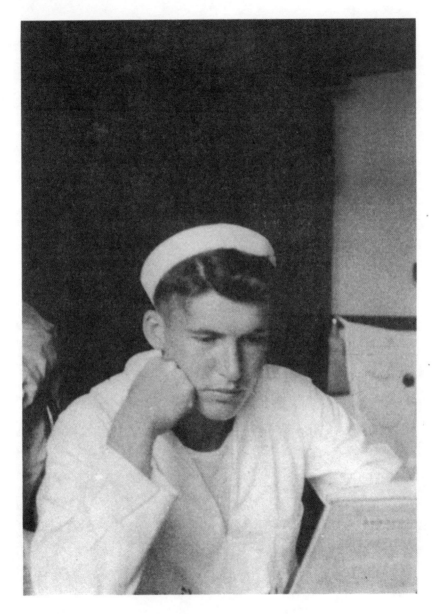

A young and studious Walter M. Schirra as a naval academy midshipman.

My makeshift plywood desk in wooden barracks at Taegu, Korea, where our base commander, Red Mason, conned us into partitioning our barracks.

Jo and I were married at the U.S. Naval Academy chapel on February 23, 1946.

Official Photograph, United States Air Force

I receive the Distinguished Flying Cross for flying combat in Korea from Major General William M. Morgan, U. S. Air Force.

Official Photograph, United States Navy

Bud Sickel and I welcome Duke Windsor to the "thousand-hour jet set."

NASA

Flying high-performance aircraft was a gratifying part of my career. Here I am pictured in the cockpit of an F-106B, the same Mach-2 aircraft I used to chase Alan Shepard during the liftoff of his suborbital flight.

The Mercury Seven with then-Vice President Richard M. Nixon.

Dee O'Hara, recipient of one of my favorite gotchas, embraces my analysis—instead of urinalysis.

Members of the original seven and the second group of nine eat iguana steak during tropic survival training in the Panama Canal Zone.

United States Air Force / NASA

Commander Walter M. Schirra, Jr.

United States Air Force/NASA

Gordo Cooper, Chris Kraft and I discuss procedures prior to the MA 8 flight.

NASA

Mercury prep with pad leader Gueuter Wendt.

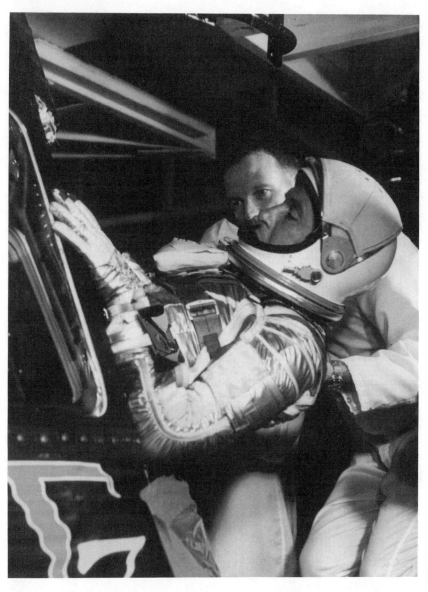

Gordo, my backup on *Sigma* 7, inserting me into the spacecraft.

NASA

NASA

Aerial view of *Kearsarge* welcoming Mercury on board.

NASA

Sigma Seven being hoisted aboard *Kearsarge*.

Who's tired here? Walt Williams and Deke Slayton greet me aboard *Kearsarge*.

NASA

Secretary of the Navy Fred Korth presents me with Naval astronaut wings as a result of my Mercury flight, while Jo looks on.

NASA

I brief President Kennedy at Complex 14 prior to my Mercury flight.

NASA

After the flight, the President entertained my family in the Oval Office.

NASA

With my parents and Mayor Wendell in Oradell, New Jersey, on October 15, 1962, the day my hometown honored me.

I share a laugh with President Johnson during Gemini training.

Early mission control at Cape Canaveral, used through Gemini 4.

NASA

Still smoking in 1966, I take a break from water egress training in the Gulf of Mexico prior to Apollo.

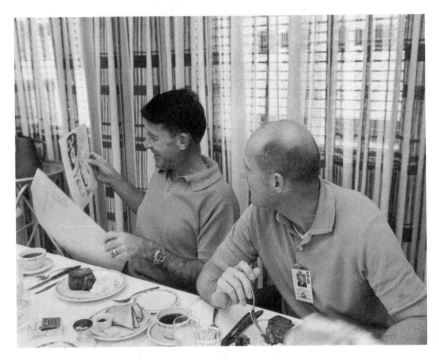

NASA

Tom Stafford and I have the traditional preflight breakfast of steak and eggs before Gemini 6.

I fiddle with my Gemini helmet.

NASA

Eight of the second nine watch my Mercury launch. John Young crouches in front; behind him, left to right: Neil Armstrong, Frank Borman, Jim Lovell, Tom Stafford, Pete Conrad (note his crossed fingers), Ed White and Jim McDivitt.

USIS

Frank Borman and I greet well-wishers in Tokyo at the beginning of our goodwill trip to Asia in 1966.

Liftoff, Apollo 7.

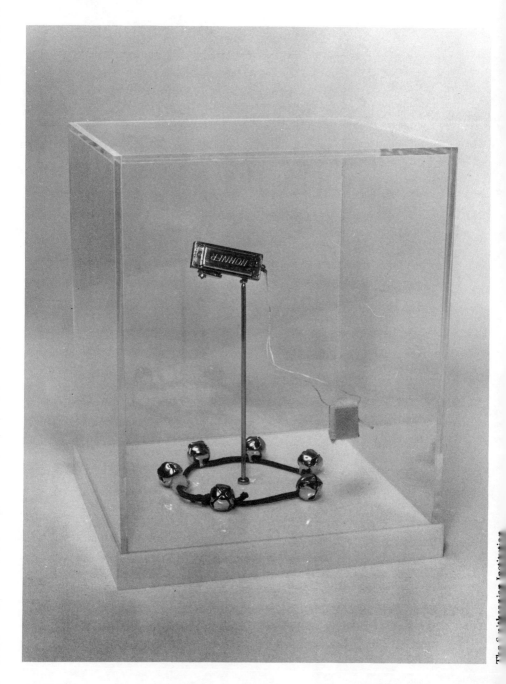

The harmonica and Christmas bells used to play "Jingle Bells" on the Gemini flight. They are now enshrined in the Smithsonian Air and Space Museum.

NASA

The first live television show from space resulted in an Emmy Award—and consternation for my secretary.

NASA

Grizzled but happy, I arrive aboard USS *Essex* with Donn Eisele and Walt Cunningham after the Apollo 7 splashdown. Survival instructor Don Stulken is on the right.

The official patch of Apollo 7.

NASA

I say a few words at The Ranch during the Presidential Awards Ceremony following Apollo 7.

Wally, Walt and Whatshisname meet the press.

June 29, 1988

The President
The White House
Washington, D. C.

Dear Mr. President:

We urge you to show your continued support for NASA and the permanently manned Space Station. We need a strong manned space program to ensure a strong country.

In 1969, when we landed on the moon, we were clearly and unquestionably the leader in space exploration. Like Columbus, we had gone beyond our world in search of the unknown. We were first. We were the best. And, we were proud to be Americans. Our advancements in space technology spurred advancements in education, commerce and industry. Our ability, our vision, and our expertise were the envy of the world.

Then, the 1970's arrived. Budget decision makers promptly forgot the successes and accomplishments of NASA and began trimming back their funding allocations. Our space program sat still, while others passed us by. You can imagine our frustration as we watch the Soviet Union take the lead in manned space flight - a lead we risked our lives to establish.

Today, we are not the same America, but we can be. Our generation has worked hard to leave a legacy for our children, for mankind. The Space Station is a continuation of that legacy. America needs the Space Station for many reasons, but perhaps the most important is that it will again establish our leadership in space.

Congress has the opportunity to approve your funding request for the Space Station. But others are fighting for the money, and Congress must understand that you really want the Space Station. Memos and staff visits are insufficient. Only your voice can make a difference. Please use your remaining days in office to visibly support our next step in space - a permanently manned Space Station.

Sincerely,

Charles Conrad
Gemini 5, Gemini 11,
Apollo 12, Skylab 2

James Lovell
Gemini 7, Gemini 12,
Apollo 8, Apollo 13

The text of a letter sent to President Reagan expressing the concerns of nineteen astronauts about the state of America's space program.

Thomas Stafford
Gemini 6, Gemini 9,
Apollo 10, Apollo 18

Neil Armstrong
Gemini 8, Apollo 11

Eugene Cernan
Gemini 9, Apollo 10,
Apollo 17

Richard Gordon
Gemini 11, Apollo 12

Walter Cunningham
Apollo 7

Alan Bean
Apollo 12, Skylab 3

Fred Haise
Apollo 13

Stuart Roosa
Apollo 14

Harrison Schmitt
Apollo 17

Joseph Kerwin
Skylab 2

Owen Garriott
Skylab 3, STS 9

Gerald Carr
Skylab 4

Edward Gibson
Skylab 4

William Pogue
Skylab 4

Donald Slayton
Apollo 18

James Irwin
Apollo 15

Walter Schirra
Mercury-Sigma 7,
Gemini 6, Apollo 7

I am awarded the title of Fellow by Bob Hoover, president of
SETP, the Society of Experimental Test Pilots.

7 Gemini: Building a Bridge to the Moon

We had come of age, suddenly. In the aftermath of Mercury's stunning success and with our sights set on a lunar landing, we were confident and full of enthusiasm. As Gemini got going, we brought together the ablest people who had learned the ropes in Mercury, astronauts and engineers who had matured together, and added a superb class of newcomers. It was a championship team.

At the management level there were changes in the making. Walt Williams was on hand for only the first Gemini flight, an unmanned test on April 8, 1964. Williams's departure was represented as a mutually beneficial career shift to the corporate sector, as Walt became a vice president of Aerospace Corporation and manager of the company's manned systems division. Actually he was shoved out in a power play, just as he had prevailed in a contest with Charlie Donlan in the early days of the Mercury program. Chris Kraft, the Mercury flight director, replaced Walt as operations director.

You live by the sword, you die by the sword, so they say. Nevertheless, we were sorry to see Walt go. He'd come to the Space Task Group when we were making the difficult transition from research

135

and development to operations. His demonstrated ability as an operations chief was a proven asset, though his brusque personality made him stand out in a crowd of engineers and scientists. Walt, fortunately, had brought with him an able senior assistant, Kenny Kleinknecht, who became deputy manager of the Gemini Program Office and later was the deputy to George Low, the director of Apollo spacecraft development. In addition to Kleinknecht, other able managers guided the Gemini effort. The Gemini project manager had been Jim Chamberlin, who was a brilliant engineer but not a successful manager. He was replaced in March 1963 by Chuck Mathews, a Space Task Group regular who'd been brought in at the outset by Bob Gilruth.

For me the most important of the people behind the scenes—the managers, engineers, technicians, etc.—was an anonymous fellow named Ralph Gendielle (pronounced Gendalee). He was the McDonnell engineer who had babied my Mercury spacecraft. We'd become very good friends, and Ralph got himself assigned to my Gemini spacecraft as well. He told me he intended to protect it. (Ralph, who died recently, was totally dedicated to the space program. When the Gemini program ended and McDonnell had not landed an Apollo contract, he quit his job and joined Grumman, the manufacturer of the lunar lander.)

Gemini's purpose was clear from the start. We had demonstrated that we could go into space and return safely. President Kennedy, having been advised that a lunar landing was feasible, had announced the United States would send men to the moon and back. So now it was necessary to prove to ourselves—to space agency officials and to the men who would make the mission—that we were capable of certain critical operations. We had to show, for example, that we could leave our spacecraft and perform tasks, depending for survival on our suit. We termed it an extravehicular activity, an EVA, though it was popularly called a spacewalk. It really wasn't a walk. In the absence of gravity it was a float. My Apollo colleagues, Neil Armstrong and others who landed on the moon, were actually the first to take steps.

We also had to prove that we could remain in space for the length of time a moon mission requried—eight days at least, though we considered two weeks a more realistic test. (Our moon landing missions, it turned out, lasted from just over eight days to twelve and a half days.)

In addition, we needed to demonstrate our ability to maneuver so precisely in space that we could rendezvous and dock. There had been a heated debate over where the event should occur en route to the moon. Wernher von Braun and his team insisted that an earth-orbit rendezvous would be more convenient in the long run, since the main terminal would be close to home, about a fifteen-minute commute. Von Braun was already thinking in terms of a permanent station in space. But it was cheaper and technically more efficient to send a lunar lander from an orbit of the moon, and that was the plan. It had been decided by the time of Gemini. In either case, if we failed to accomplish the rendezvous and docking, it would ruin our entire day.

Finally, we would have an opportunity to make pinpoint landings in Gemini. An onboard computer was required for rendezvous, and we would also use it for a precisely controlled re-entry. The computer would control the lift vector, the angle of the re-entry and the velocity. The vector in turn would determine the landing area—the footprint, as it's known.

The footprint was calculated by ground computers during our Mercury missions, but there were other factors—retrofire time and spacecraft attitude were the main ones—affecting our point of return. I was so totally resolved to making a spot-on landing that I practiced re-entry over and over in the simulator at Langley. I kept missing—by 3.9 miles, then 4.1, 3.8, 4.2 and so on. After my Mercury flight I checked charts and navigation data, and I concluded that they were in error. The Australia land mass, my last earth fix prior to retrofire, was four miles out of position.

My findings were confirmed in the Gemini missions, and we found it necessary to reorient the tracking network—to tell the stations where they were.

On most of the Gemini missions we landed in the designated area—on all but one in fact. That was Gemini 8, piloted by Neil Armstrong with Dave Scott, who joined the program with the third group of astronauts in 1963. The flight was called "the whirligig," because the spacecraft developed a high rate of spin in a docking exercise. Armstrong and Scott were recovered safely after an emergency landing out near Okinawa, which caused some anxious moments.

As we had in Mercury, we anticipated landing in some places far off the beaten track. We trained for such a contingency. Since we wouldn't fly a polar orbit we didn't worry about coping with an arctic enviroment. However, coming down in a tropical forest was a possibility. So all sixteen astronauts went to Panama where the Air Force runs a jungle survival facility.

We had no escape tower in Gemini, as we had in Mercury and would again in Apollo, but we had ejection seats. In the event of a land landing, we would come down by parachute, wearing a space suit and equipped with a raft and survival kit. Since we'd be flying in pairs, we were teamed in training. My partner in Panama was Jim McDivitt, later commander of the second Gemini mission. Delivered by helicopter, we camped beside a stream for several days in conditions not nearly so harsh as on the Nevada desert. We ate iguana and the heart of a palm tree, which ruined my taste for hearts of palm salad for years. We also fished, but without success.

Since the stream wasn't a source of food, I decided to mark our position by coloring the water with sea dye. Each day we dumped in more dye, not fully appreciating our colleagues' reaction downstream. As helicopters dropped food and supplies to our camp, marking the point of origin of the dye-marker, we began receiving disgruntled visitors, who had trekked for miles through the tropical forest. Tom Stafford and Gene Cernan, just downstream from McDivitt and me, were more astonished than angry. They'd been trying to fish, I learned later, when all of a sudden the river turned chartreuse.

Listening To Leo

From time to time questions have been raised about the astronauts' business affairs, beginning with the *Life* magazine payments for our personal stories. The White House approved those payments and they continued in Gemini. Eyebrows were raised, however, by rumors of payola and by our investments.

The rumors were unfounded, pure and simple. As for our investments, they were scrutinized by NASA officials, including James E. Webb, the administrator.

In Febuary 1962 we were in Washington to celebrate John Glenn's Mercury flight. At a dignitary lunch I was seated with Lady Bird

138

Johnson, Albert Thomas, congressman from Houston, and Jim Webb. They started talking about good old Texas hospitality and how the folks in Houston would welcome the astronauts in real style. In fact a fellow named Frank Sharp, who was developing a community called Sharpstown, was going to give us fully furnished new homes. It was a tempting offer, but Leo DeOrsey, our financial adviser, said no dice. He said it was wrong, and that was that. We all bought homes instead.

Then there was the controversy over the Corvettes. Al Shepard loved to drive those Chevrolet sports models. Through Al we met Jim Rathmann, a Cadillac-Chevrolet dealer in Melbourne, Florida, near Cape Canaveral. Rathmann was a race car driver, winner of the Indianapolis 500 in 1960 and a three-time runner-up. He became a good friend of Al, Gus, Gordo and me.

Through Rathmann we ended up driving Corvettes. They were loaners, "brass hat cars," meaning we drove them for a year and either bought them or returned them to General Motors. It was a common automotive industry practice to loan cars and then sell them as "executive driven." G.M. loaned cars to VIPs because it was good promotion. However, when the press made an issue of our driving free automobiles, as if it were a crime, we dug in our heels and said to hell with the press.

When we had the meeting with DeOrsey about the houses in Houston, he said, "As for those cars, don't worry about it. It doesn't matter." And I said, "Well, actually, Leo, I don't like Corvettes anyway."

I meant it. I had been driving an Austin-Healey, a British roadster, before I got the Corvette, and was used to driving with a light touch. The Corvette, to me, was a brute force car. I thought of an automobile as I did an aircraft or a spacecraft. I wanted to feel I was a part of the machine, able to guide it with the push of my finger or the flick of my wrist. I returned the Corvette and bought a Maserati.

The story of the Cape Colony Inn is sad, and again I blame the press. We weren't supposed to be sophisticated or astute, for that would contradict the image. We were just dumb pilots, the Rover Boys in space.

Leo DeOrsey had proposed to us that we build a motel in Cocoa Beach. As an owner of the Kenilworth in Miami Beach, Leo knew the value of hotel investments in Florida. He put the package together. Each of us would put in about $10,000, making us minority stockholders with a total share of less than 50 percent. Leo brought in as major owner a hotel developer named Tom Rose. Henri Landwirth, also a part-owner, quit his job at the Holiday Inn to become the manager. We named the motel the Cape Colony Inn.

The press raised the question of a conflict of interest. That was hard to take, believe me. We made no secret of the deal—in fact, many of the major news organizations rented space in an office complex at the Cape Colony. Leo told us to ignore it. "People are pushing you who don't have a right to push you," he said. "They're making a living out of the space program. You guys are doing the space program and not making a living of it."

The motel didn't do as well as we had hoped, and Leo suggested we sell. "The press is harassing you, so let them think they won," he said. We doubled our money and put it elsewhere—in an apartment complex in Virginia and in some land in Lakeland, Florida, with Landwirth. End of story, almost. Henri had to leave Cocoa Beach because of a no-compete clause in the contract to sell the Cape Colony. He and John Glenn later became partners, and today they own two very profitable Holiday Inns adjacent to Disney World in Orlando.

Fun And Gamesmanship

In our everyday relations with each other we were loyal above all. We were spontaneous, quick to criticize if need be, always ready to laugh at a wisecrack. We had no place for soreheads, and any angry outburst was met with advice to cool it. We were competitive, of course, but we expressed it in the spirit of camaraderie. We each figured we were the best in our business, but assertions of superiority were in keeping with our mutual respect. We kidded each other a lot. The seven of us who had come through Mercury were very close, and we were rapidly assimilating the Gemini guys. In addition to Pete Conrad and Jim Lovell, my old Navy pals, I had come to admire a couple of Air Force pilots, Jim McDivitt and Tom Stafford. Stafford, an Annapolis graduate, was to be the pilot of the Gemini flight I commanded.

Some of the teasing, not much, had to do with the missions. As it turned out, I made three flights and logged about twelve days in space—a little under a day in Mercury, a little over a day in Gemini, and almost eleven days in Apollo. By the time I retired, Al Shepard had made only his Mercury suborbital flight, and I reminded him that his flight time of fifteen minutes amounted to what it had taken me to return from orbit on each of my three flights. Al finally topped me by going to the moon. I needled Gus Grissom the same way. His Gemini three-orbit flight, plus his Mercury suborbital, came to just over five hours.

Gus was a fierce competitor, however. He established his turf. He was first in Gemini, and he was the commander of the first Apollo mission when he was killed. He had also planned on being the first of us to land on the moon.

Gus was also something of a gotcha champion, especially in those involving cars. He once really nailed Shepard, which was no mean feat. This was at the cape, I'd say in 1964. Gus and Al each had new Corvettes. They would drive in formation as if they were doing engineering test flights, comparing data. Al would hold up three fingers for 3,000 r.p.m., Gus would nod and off they'd go. Or they would stop for a light side by side and roar off together as if on a drag strip. Every time Gus would leave Al in the dust. Why? Simple. He had gotten Jim Rathmann to increase his gear ratio, so it would produce 4,000 r.p.m.,compared to the standard 3,000 r.p.m. of Shepard's car. More r.p.m. increases acceleration, while it reduces top speed.

Shepard was furious. He was Mr. Corvette, after all. He couldn't believe Gus's car was that much better. Immediately he went to Rathmann's shop for a tune-up. Jim of course kept the car for a day and did nothing. Shepard lost again to Gus and returned to the shop. Didn't Rathmann have a mechanic who had worked on his car at Indianapolis? Rathmann said he'd done all he could. Al finally figured it out and laughed it off, but he didn't think it was very funny.

Occasionally, we ran afoul of the law. Our white Corvettes were easy to spot, and who could blame a traffic cop for wanting to boast about writing up an astronaut? Once we made news. Alan Shepard, the first American in space, had been arrested for speeding in Orlando. Al had been caught while racing with a Triumph, a TR3, driven by a young gal. She passed him, and Al couldn't resist the challenge. We got a TR3 decal and put it on Al's car, the way fighter pilots decorate their cockpits with the insignia of downed enemy aircraft. And we added a few decals—two Volkswagens and three Schwinn bicycles, as I recall. Even though he was the victim, Al enjoyed that one as much as the rest of us.

Now my favorite traffic cop story. Al and Gus and I were at the North American plant in Downey, California, in 1966. It was an early stage of the Apollo program, and North American was the spacecraft contractor. Gus had gotten to know another race car driver, Carroll Shelby, and had borrowed his monster car, a Shelby Mustang. Designed so Ford could compete with the G.M. Corvette, it would do 130 m.p.h.

During the lunch break one day Gus suggested to Al and me that we take the Shelby for a spin. Al took the wheel and I slid into the passenger seat. We drove out onto a six-lane suburban street. It was a shopping area with cars parked on either side of the street but almost no moving traffic. It was a suitable spot for a zero-to- sixty acceleration test.

"Stand by," I said, checking my watch, as Shepard warmed up the engine. "Stand by, mark." We took off, tires screeching, and just as we hit sixty, Shepard shouted, "Oh, shit!" He slammed on the brakes as I spotted the flashing light of a patrol car. Shepard got out and greeted two officers, who were laughing themselves silly.

"You're Al Shepard, aren't you?"

"That's right."

"And who's that in the car? Is that Wally Schirra?"

"Yes, sir."

"Well,that was a pretty dumb thing you just did, Mr. Shepard. If you're going to do a zero-to-sixty check in a Shelby Mustang, don't do it when you're sitting next to a police car."

That was that. We were lucky they didn't give us a ticket. Later we laughed too. It told us something about ourselves. So intent were we about the car's performance that our attention was focused on the speedometer, my stopwatch and the road ahead. Such a fixation was typical of the seven of us.

Our affinity for race drivers isn't difficult to explain. Rathmann and Shelby were also in a high-risk profession. They put their lives on the line doing what we called their low-altitude orbits. Also, in any intensely competitive field the players are likely to try to one-up one another whenever they can. I gather golfers on the pro tour are pretty good at playing gotcha.

When we came back from jungle survival training in Panama we brought a baby boa constrictor for Rathmann, who is deathly fearful of snakes. Shepard, Grissom and Cooper wrapped it in cheesecloth and took it to his dealership in Melbourne. When they walked into his office, Rathmann bolted out the back door. Returning in a few minutes, Rathmann shrugged it off and said he had a pet of his own he'd like to show them.

In the back of his parts shop Rathmann had a wooden box about a foot square by two feet long with heavy-gauge chicken wire on one side, a padlocked door, and words of warning stenciled on it: DANGER—LIVE INDIAN MONGOOSE—DO NOT TOUCH. As Shepard watched warily from one side, Grissom and Cooper were beautifully victimized. Rathmann tapped on the box trying to arouse the mongoose, and Gus peered in through the wire. Gordo held the baby boa up to the screen to see if the mongoose would react. Of course, the padlock was for show. The door was held by a hook, and when Rathmann flipped it with his finger, a foxtail was released by a spring. Gordo jumped three feet into the air and flung the boa constrictor at Gus. To keep it from wrapping itself around his neck, Gus threw the snake into the air. The foxtail landed on a table where Shepard was sitting, and Al started hitting the furry thing with a hammer. Rathmann laughed so hard that he fell against a parts bin, knocking it over and starting a domino reaction of crashing bins.

There's a twenty-second segment in the movie *The Right Stuff* of me doing the mongoose trick. I get credit for it, but that's wrong. I've pulled it since, but it was Rathmann's idea, and he does it deftly. You must aim the box so the foxtail shoots right through the victim's legs, and you remind him that the mongoose attacks a man at the genitals. That's how Rathmann really got Cooper.

I bought my Maserati in the spring of 1965. It was second-hand, about a year old. Its owner had brought it to Daytona Beach for the auto races, and Rathmann had learned it was for sale. He arranged the transaction, even while he didn't conceal his distaste for Italian cars. He called them spaghetti bowls. Then he sat down with Grissom over a drink and formulated a plan. "We've got to get Schirra," he said to Gus. "He's ready. He thinks Italian cars are the neatest in the world. He'll believe about anything you tell him."

143

Gus set the bait. He told me that he couldn't decide whether to purchase the Corvette he'd had on loan or to buy a sleek, beautiful Ferrari that would cost about the same as the Corvette.

"Wait a minute, Gus," I said. "You've got a really good deal."

"Yeah, I know."

"A Corvette is only $6,000. You can get a Ferrari for $6,000?"

"Yeah, I know it's a good deal."

A new Ferrari was worth about $15,000. I kept thinking about what Gus had told me. He played me along skillfully. I advised him to have the car checked by a good mechanic. He could spend a fortune on the Ferrari if it wasn't in good running condition.

We were getting ready for my Gemini mission with Gus working with me as the backup commander. Gus told me I was getting too agitated thinking about the Ferrari. He was right.

"Gus, have you closed the deal?" My tone was impatient.

"No, I'm still thinking about that Vette."

"Gus, for God's sake don't let the Ferrari get away. Let me know. I'll sell my Maserati. I'd love that Ferrari."

A couple of days later, after Grissom and Rathmann had decided they had carried the joke too far, Gus said to me, "I'm not going to buy the Ferrari, Wally. I told the guy to forget it."

"Where the hell is it?" I demanded. "Whats the guy's name?"

Gus wouldn't tell me, of course. I then telephoned Rathmann, who said the car had been sold to somone in Orlando. I was destroyed. "What's the name of the guy who bought it?" I asked Rathmann. "Maybe he doesn't realize how much it's worth."

That's when Gus told me I'd been on the hook for two months. "I've got to tell you, Wally. We're afraid you'll have a breakdown before your flight."

Gus was the master of the ruse. He was driving back from dinner one night in his Corvette with Jim Rathmann, going from our new crew quarters at the Kennedy Space Center on Merritt Island to A1A, the highway that leads down the coast to Cocoa Beach and Melbourne. The route runs across a causeway to Port Canaveral, and there's a long bend just as you're leaving the government reservation. We could go pretty fast out there late at night. The area was patrolled by federal security guards who weren't inclined to be traffic police.

Gus said to Rathmann as they hit the bend, "I don't know why, but I can do only sixty-five, maybe seventy, on this turn. Wally goes through here at eighty. I've seen him do it. It must be that Italian car." Rathmann was sucked right in. "Let me try," he said. With the former Indy 500 winner behind the wheel, they came roaring through the turn at eighty, out of control. By the time they stopped, they were two hundred feet off the highway mired in the mud. The car had to be towed, and it was a mess, but Gus enjoyed every minute of it.

Ray Firestone, then the president of Firestone Tire and Rubber, was a friend of Jim Rathmann's and came to the cape for my Gemini flight in October 1965. The night before the scheduled launch we had dinner at the crew quarters—Ray, Jim, Gus and I.

During the dinner Firestone said, "Wally if you pull off this rendezvous tomorrow, I'll give you a set of tires for your car." The mission that Tom Stafford and I were to fly the following day called for a rendezvous and docking with the Agena stage of an Atlas-Agena rocket that would go off just ahead of us. I said thanks, but I reminded Ray that Firestone tires did not fit the wheels of my Maserati. "Well then," he said, "I'll also give you a set of Borani wheels. If you do the rendezvous, you'll find five wheels and tires plus new brakes when you get back to Houston." Boranis were expensive Italian spoked wheels. "Sounds terrific," I said.

Actually, I was overwhelmed. A Borani wheel was then worth about $500, so this was a $3,000 gift. I should have suspected there was a rub, but I didn't. Firestone and Rathmann intended to include a sixth wheel in the shipment, one that had been pounded until it was slightly oval shaped, so my car would ride with an inexplicable bounce.

We didn't launch as planned on October 25, 1965, because the Agena blew up before reaching orbit. We finally did go on December 15, and the mission was a success. We rendezvoused with Gemini 7, flown by Frank Borman and Jim Lovell. Firestone and Rathmann again came out for dinner on the night before launch, with Ray repeating his offer. Again I said fine.

Back in Houston after the mission I got word from the Firestone office that the wheels and tires were there. I had them put on my Maserati and drove off, pleased with their appearance. What I didn't know was the oval wheel was never shipped. By mistake the two Borani wheels on the rear were reversed at the Firestone shop. Screwed on backwards they proceeded to wind loose. I was driving past the Manned Spacecraft Center on my way home when I saw a wheel roll into a ditch. I didn't realize it was mine until my Maserati lurched to one side and slid to a stop. So the planned gotcha didn't happen, but I had become the victim of an unplanned gotcha.

I got home on the spare, but the wheel was ruined. I called Rathmann and said I was embarrassed to ask Firestone for another Borani. Jim said he'd take care of it. A week or so later a package arrived at the airport, nine dollars C.O.D. from Melbourne, Florida. I picked it up, certain it was the new wheel. When I got it home and opened the crate, I found a rusty, grungy wheel for, I believe, a 1928 Essex. On the hubcap was a label—Messy Roddy—and the old worn tire was a Badrich, in tribute to a prominent Firestone competitor.

I quickly closed the garage door, so no one could see, especially Grissom, who was my next-door neighbor. I nailed the crate shut, put it in Jo's station wagon, and took it to the dump. A few days later the new wheel arrived, and the Maserati was running fine again. That was that. I never said a word about it, and Rathmann never asked. That's how you handle a gotcha.

That same winter Gordo Cooper and I went to Daytona Beach with Rathmann to see a race and stay overnight. I was aching to score one on Jim, who no doubt suspected as much. Jim, Gordo, one of Jim's managers and I flew up in Jim's plane, a twin-engine Navion four-seater. On the return flight Rathmann suggested I take the controls, and I agreed.

We landed at Titusville, Florida, where Gordo and I had left our rented car. I got out, unlocked the baggage compartment and got our bags, and as we walked to the car, I handed the keys to Jim's manager and said, "Don't tell Jim you have these for a very long time." Of course, one of the keys would be needed to start up the airplane. As Gordo and I drove off, I watched Jim in the mirror. He started the pat-the-pocket routine, and I could almost read his thoughts. He was saying to himself, "Those dumb bastards have taken my keys!" He started running behind us, but we were gone. Naturally, when he got back to the plane his manager would say, "Oh, were you looking for these?"

I had actually owned a Ferrari by the time Gus conned me into believing there was one for sale for $6,000. I bought it in 1963, not long after my Mercury mission. I began to yield to temptation while I was getting ready for Gemini at the McDonnell plant in St. Louis. A dealer there sold "pre-owned Ferraris" for well under the $15,000 price tag for new models. Mine had supposedly been owned by Brigitte Bardot. It was red but not really wild. I never liked the car and got rid of it in less than a year.

I got the Ferrari shined up and took it to Houston. I didn't know it, but a plot was in an advanced planning stage. Even Jo was in on it. The astronauts and their wives had had it with my incessant talk about Italian cars. The plot began on the first day I drove the Ferrari to the Manned Spacecraft Center. Jo called ahead to the office saying, "Wally is on his way."

I parked in our lot, and I walked into the Spacecraft Center. As I ambled down the corridor Gordo Cooper called me into his office and pointed out the window. "Is that your car?" he said. I said, "Yeah." I looked down and saw a magnificent Ferrari approaching. Built to be driven only on the track, it was an ultimate racing machine. My colleagues had borrowed it from John Mecom, Jr., an oilman and sportsman we'd all come to know. At the wheel was Al Shepard, who blithely stepped out, smoothed his hair, and reached for his attaché case. He walked in, never looking up. Of course, he had parked next to my Ferrari. Suddenly I felt like I was driving a Model T. I was put in my place without a word being spoken.

Some gotchas were not so successful. At about the same time of the Ferrari I bought a Cal 25 sailboat, built in California. I had talked about sailing a lot, having just switched from power boats. A plan was devised to get me for my motor mouth by removing my boat from its slip at the yacht club on Clear Lake and hiding it. Then my friends would stick a mast in the mud, so I would believe my boat had sunk. Without knowing it I outfoxed them. I returned from Cape Canaveral before they could pull it off. It was a gotcha that never happened, and it cost them a few bucks since they'd bought a Cal 25 mast.

We gathered at the Indianapolis 500 in 1967. Jim Rathmann had retired as a driver, but he still had the bug, and Gordo Cooper had caught it. Gordo and Pete Conrad had gone to race driving school and had become certified by the Sports Car Club of America (SCCA). Rathmann and Cooper jointly owned a car they intended to enter, if they could get it qualified.

I had become a friend by this time of the great driver, A. J. Foyt, who lived in in Houston. A. J. had a stable of Ford Coyotes entered in 1967, eventually winning the race in one of them. During the qualifying trials A. J. and I were eating sandwiches in his shop when he made a proposal. "You know Wally, I've got three cars in this race. I understand Rathmann and Cooper have a car they're hoping to enter. Would you like to be an owner too?"

Jim and Gordo were out there busting their butts, and they never did get their car qualified. They were working on the engine with the pit crew when they heard an announcement on the public address system.

"Coyote car qualified. Schirra owner."

Rathmann came running up to me, and boy was he livid. "How the hell did you do this?," he shouted.

I wasn't really the owner, but Rathmann believed it. Gotcha.

TEN MISSIONS IN TWO YEARS

After two unmanned tests, in April 1964 and January 1965, the Titan II launch vehicle and the Gemini spacecraft had been proved worthy. We began manned missions with Gemini 3, which was launched on March 23, 1965. In ten missions in 1965 and 1966 we logged 970 hours in space. We had some scary moments, but we completed the Gemini program without a serious accident. It was during Gemini that we made an operational transfer. When Gus Grissom and John Young flew Gemini 3, Mission Control was at Cape Canaveral, but the remaining flights were directed from the Manned Spacecraft Center in Houston.

As we progressed, we grew in many ways, not all of them for the better. The number of people in the space program had multiplied since the early days of Mercury, and that became the reason for a vast security system. It was ridiculous. I had to carry ten badges to pass through checkpoints at the Kennedy Space Center and out on the cape itself, where the launch pad was still located.

As the backups on Gemini 3, Stafford and I were were at the pad prior to launch. When Grissom and Young arrived in the immaculate white suits we used in Gemini, I greeted them wearing an old Mercury training suit. Its silver coating was tarnished, and while it was already tattered, I'd cut holes until it was almost falling apart. Around my neck I had about twenty security badges that dangled down to the floor. "If you're not feeling up to it," I said to Gus,

"I'll be happy to take this one." He cracked up.

The three-orbit flight of Gemini 3 was a total success. Gus had named the spacecraft Molly Brown, as in the unsinkable, for he still sought vindication for the mishap on his Mercury mission. As luck would have it, the Gemini 3 spacecraft was dragged beneath the surface by its parachute after splashdown, and Gus had reason to fear for a moment that they might be going down.

There was an unfortunate flap after the Gemini 3 mission, and while Young was blamed, I'll now confess it was my fault. The cause: a corned beef sandwich.

Young mentioned to me a day or so before launch that there was not a meal scheduled on the flight, since the flight was less than five hours. But add a two-and-a-half-hour countdown, he reasoned, and they were bound to get hungry. So I went to Wolfie's, a restaurant and deli in Cocoa Beach, and bought a corned beef sandwich on rye with two dill pickle slices. I kept it in a refrigerator in the crew quarters and got word to Young that it was there. John tucked the sandwich into his space suit, and when Gus complained of being hungry during the flight, he said, "We have it taken care of, sir."

The doctors complained about an unconventional diet, which was nonsense, but some reporters heard of the incident and blew it out of proportion, as usual. Little did they know this was not a first for such antics. When I flew in Mercury and Cooper was my backup, Gordo put a special rations kit in the spacecraft. It contained a steak sandwich, a two-ounce bottle of Scotch and five cigarettes. My restraint harness prevented me from reaching the goodies, or I might have eaten the sandwich. Smoking and drinking, of course, were forbidden.

Young was mildly rebuked, but his career was unaffected. He later commanded a Gemini mission, Gemini 10, flew twice in Apollo, leading the fifth lunar-landing mission, and was the first space shuttle commander.

Jim McDivitt and Ed White flew Gemini 4 on June 3, 1965. White was the first American to leave an orbiting spacecraft. A Russian, Alexi Leonov, had accomplished the first EVA in March. White's "spacewalk" was the cause of some anxiety, as usual more for us on the ground than for the crew. White seemed to lose track of time. He had been outside the spacecraft for more than fifteen minutes when Chris Kraft, the mission director, sent an order to McDivitt:

"Tell him to get back in." White obeyed, but he had difficulty closing the hatch, and when finally settled in his seat, he was exhausted.

Gordon Cooper and Pete Conrad were aboard Gemini 5 when it lifted off August 21 on what was to be the longest flight to date. Gordo had wanted to name the spacecraft Covered Wagon and use as a mission motto "Eight days or bust." Jim Webb didn't like the idea that anything short of eight days would be a "bust" and said no. NASA banned the naming of spacecraft for the rest of the Gemini program.

Gemini 5 was a troubled flight. In its early hours the supply of oxygen and hydrogen to a fuel cell, which was being used as a source of power for the first time, dropped dangerously due to a faulty heater. Kraft considered terminating the mission, but the problem stabilized. During these hours of uncertainty, Gordo sketched on the deck of the spacecraft next to his seat a covered wagon hanging precariously on the edge of a cliff.

At the end of five days the OAMS, the orbital attitude and maneuvering system, went on the blink. Gordo and Pete drifted throughout the rest of the mission. They had nothing to do but endure, and Pete wished he had brought a book. After 190 hours 55 minutes and 14 seconds Gemini 5 landed eighty miles short of its target in the Atlantic. Cooper had recognized a programming error in the computer and had compensated for it with manual controls. Otherwise the splashdown would have been farther still from the recovery ships.

The final two flights of 1965 were Gemini 6 and 7, launched within eleven days of each other in December. Gemini 7, with Frank Borman and Jim Lovell, went first on a two-week endurance test. Tom Stafford and I followed in Gemini 6. We were able to use Gemini 7 as our rendezvous target.

There were five Gemini missions in 1966, beginning with Armstrong and Scott aboard Gemini 8, "the whirligig," in March. Gemini 9 flew in June with Tom Stafford as the commander and Gene Cernan as the pilot. They rendezvoused with an Agena, and Cernan did a two-hour EVA. On Gemini 10 in July John Young and Mike Collins rendezvoused with two Agenas, and Collins did two EVAs. On Gemini 11 in September Pete Conrad and Dick Gordon rendezvoused and docked, and Gordon did an EVA. On Gemini 12 in November Jim Lovell and Buzz Aldrin docked three times, and Aldrin's three EVAs totalled five hours 37 minutes, a record.

No Mercury astronauts flew in 1966. The commanders of the flights were all from the second group, named in 1962, and the pilots had all come aboard in 1963. Overall sixteen astronauts filled twenty Gemini slots—Young, Conrad, Stafford and Lovell all flew twice. Of the sixteen, thirteen would fly Apollo.

Three would not. Gus Grissom and Ed White died in a spacecraft fire on the launch pad. Gordon Cooper was out of favor with the higher-ups. His Mercury mission had been a great success, and nothing that went wrong on Gemini 5 could be blamed on him. Yet he was passed over. Gordo's last assignment was as the backup commander of Gemini 12. He was pretty bitter by then.

GETTING READY FOR GEMINI 6

It was okay with me not to name the spacecraft. Names seem to me to be irrelevant to the purpose of a mission. I had, however, thought about a patch for Gemini 6 featuring the constellation Orion. Tom Stafford and I planned to do our rendezvous with Orion as a guide in our field of view. The patch would be six-sided, since six was the number of our mission. Orion also appears in the first six hours of right ascension in astronomical terms, a quarter of the way around the celestial sphere.

Gemini 6 was the last of the short-duration missions. We flew on old-fashioned batteries, not a fuel cell, a device that combines oxygen and hydrogen to produce a free electron that provides electricity. It also creates H_2O, or water, as a by-product. With an abundance of water we began to try a variety of freeze-dried foods. But that came later. Simple as it was, the fuel cell was still being perfected in 1965, as indicated by its malfunction on the Gemini 5 mission.

Our mission was to do a rendezvous, a difficult task. Frankly, in those days we didn't know how to do a rendezvous. Buzz Aldrin gave us an academic approach. A West Point graduate who had an advanced degree in science and astronautics from MIT, he was our doctor of rendezvous. Buzz advocated the Hohmann Transfer, so named for Walter Hohmann, a scientist who plotted it in 1925. On paper the Hohmann Transfer looks great. It's a perfect maneuver in earth orbit, meaning you traverse the earth once and return to a predicted point. The rendezvous is achieved in one-half of a revolution, 180 degrees. It's the most efficient, quickest and prettiest way to do a rendezvous. But it is intolerant of error. If you blow the rendezvous, fuel and time constraints won't permit another try.

We worked on rendezvous in the spacecraft simulator at McDonnell in St. Louis, an electronic facility in a computer complex. Stafford and I practiced maneuvers over and over and plotted them on little boards. We were commuting regularly to St. Louis and had apartments there. Dean Grimm, an engineer from the Manned Spacecraft Center in Houston, gave us great help. We opted to do the rendezvous during 270 degrees of rotation, which offered a much greater chance of success. We knew that when we went to the moon in Apollo, we would be doing a rendezvous in lunar orbit. The crew's survival hinged on its success.

In our simulations we assumed our target would be in a circular orbit at a given altitude. Our spacecraft would be in a lower elliptical orbit and would be able to catch the target. It was our job, using a computer, to determine the flight profiles that would enable the spacecraft to intercept the target.

Stafford and I did some fifty rendezvous simulations in St. Louis, and there were side benefits in terms of what we learned. For example, we found that we both objected to doing the rendezvous with our spacecraft in a head-toward-earth position because it meant switching back and forth from visual to electronic references. We found we lost our sense of direction doing it that way, same as an airplane pilot who tries to switch from visual to instrument flight rules.

We also spent many hours rehearsing the docking maneuver in a trainer in Houston. Housed in a six-story building, it consisted of a full-scale Gemini cockpit and the docking adapter of the Agena. They were two separate vehicles in an air-drive system that moved back and forth free of friction. We exerted control in the cockpit with small thrusters, identical to those on the spacecraft. We could go up and down, left and right, back and forth. The target could be maneuvered in those planes as well, though it was inert. It would move if we pushed against it, just as we assumed the Agena would do in space. We would close with the target at about a foot per second, an ideal velocity, and try to make contact with enough impact to secure the latches.

As a rule we practiced alone. There was no need for a copilot, since it was eyeball work. But once I was joined in the trainer by Hubert Humphrey, then vice president of the United States. The astronauts knew Humphrey from our trips to Washington. We usually stayed at the Georgetown Inn because its manager, Collins Bird, was a friend. Collins knew Humphrey, and on a number of occasions he would join us at the inn. We'd gather in a back room to have a few drinks and chat. Invariably the vice president would play the bass fiddle, taking turns with Collins Bird.

One day my secretary was in a tizzy over a call from Washington. The vice president was on the line. "Wally" he said, "I plan to visit your center, and I'd like to take a ride in your docking trainer." I said of course. Well, he did come down on an official tour. I was in the trainer, holding it stable, and as everyone watched, the vice president climbed the ladder and came aboard. He sat in the copilot's seat, and I secured the hatch. When the lights in the complex were dimmed, as they normally were while we trained, Mr. Humphrey asked me if his voice could be heard outside the trainer. I clicked off my radio and said, "No, sir." The he asked, "Do you mind if I go to sleep while you do your deal?" He proceeded to doze off for ten minutes, and when he woke he made one more request. "Now explain what you've been doing so I can tell those people down below."

I was a fan of Hubert Humphrey from that day on.

We were moving right along in Gemini. We had made a smooth transition from the Atlas booster used in Mercury to the more powerful Titan II. We had adapted well to the Gemini spacecraft, which was a much more sophisticated machine than the Mercury model, weighing almost three times as much. In Gemini we could fire the OAMS and alter our orbit, not just our attitude as we did in Mercury. And we had the onboard computer to tell us the characteristics of our orbit—its apogee or high point and its perigee or low point.

An elementary example of orbital mechanics ought to illustrate how we used the computer. Assume an elliptical orbit with an apogee of 200 miles and a perigee of 150 miles. If we increased our velocity by one foot per second at the perigee, we would add a mile of altitude at the apogee. The computer would make the measurements precisely, recording the change in velocity and indicating the new altitudes at apogee and perigee. We could take that data and determine longitudinal change, meaning the shift fore and aft in relation to the orbital plane and the side motion out of the plane.

153

With this ability to plot our orbit we could readily compare it to the orbit of the target vehicle.

Relative position isn't necessarily measured in terms of an entire orbit. We were able to keep track of where we were in space by knowing our vector. A vector is an arrow suspended in space. Its length is the velocity, its direction is the heading. It's length is changed by an increase or decrease in velocity. Its direction is changed by making left-right or up-down moves. The computer kept track of position by constantly recording the vector.

Another way to show how we altered our orbit is to hark back to an explanation of how we got into orbit in the first place. Imagine it this way. You throw a stone, and it makes an arc and falls to earth. You fire a rifle into the air, and the bullet also makes an arc and lands on earth, though at a greater distance. If you were able to fire the rifle with great power and the bullet went fast enough and far enough, the bullet would continue to fall without hitting the ground. The curvature of the earth would prevent it from making impact, and it would fall all the way around the earth. That bullet would be in earth orbit. When we are in orbit, we are in a continual fall.

Technically, you send an object into orbit when you balance the centripetal force that causes it to return to earth with sufficient centrifugal force to drive it away from earth. Remember the bucket of water that stayed full when you swung it in a circle? You were demonstrating the orbital principle, a balancing of centripetal and centrifugal forces. We unbalance those forces slightly to change orbit. We unbalance them to a greater degree when we fire retrorockets to re-enter the atmosphere. Of course, the balance of forces is critical. It would become more so on flights returning from the moon.

We were so pleased with our progress that we were needling the people at North American, the contractor for the Apollo spacecraft. We told them they'd better get off their asses, or we'd be going around the moon with Gemini. Our warning wasn't entirely in jest. In 1965 a proposal for a large earth orbit, a LEO, was endorsed by MSC officials, including Dr. Gilruth. A Gemini spacecraft in large earth orbit would circle around the moon. Thus Americans would fly in the vicinity of the moon, though they would not be able to land. The LEO idea was vetoed by NASA headquarters in Washington.

As launch day for Gemini 6 grew near, the attitude of the crew—
Tom Stafford and I and our backups, Gus Grissom and John Young—
turned serious. We began to think about the variables. We felt good
about the Titan II, since it had successfully launched three Gemini
flights. And we trusted the Atlas, the old Mercury beast. We knew
little about the Agena, however. It was a liquid propellant second-
stage vehicle that was to be inserted into orbit by the Atlas and
become our rendezvous target. Built by Lockheed, the Agena had
been used to send satellites such as those of Discoverer, an Air Force
reconnaissance program, into a high orbit. We were hoping to communicate with the Agena electronically and to use its engine to
propel the Gemini 6 spacecraft. The potential of the Agena was
tremendous. We were just starting to utilize big and powerful systems in space, the sort of systems that eventually would take us to
the moon.

8 Gemini: The Rendezvous

SALVO LAUNCH—AN IDEA EVOLVES

As I review a flying career of twenty-odd years, I can recall a few memorable moments in which I approached the ultimate flying experience. My first carrier landing in the F8F Bearcat was one. Another was the test flights of the F4H Phantom II at Edwards Air Force Base in California. Test pilots describe their reaction to the performance of an aircraft in terms of the harmony that develops between a man and a machine. If you ever achieve exquisite harmony, you have reached a level of absolute confidence. Man and machine have become one. There is no limit to what they can do together.

Perhaps exquisite harmony is just beyond our reach. That's the way it ought to be, I suspect. But I came closest during the Gemini 6 mission. It was when we succeeded in doing the rendezvous. I was at the controls of the Gemini spacecraft. I had brought her to within inches of the target, another spacecraft, Gemini 7. I was cavorting about, flying rings around Gemini 7.

My Gemini spacecraft was the orbital equivalent of a fighter aircraft. It was stripped to the essentials of a twenty-six-hour mission. And just as I had a radar observer in the Phantom II, I had Tom Stafford in the

157

right-side seat. We were so tightly crammed into the cockpit we could literally say that instead of climbing into the spacecraft, we had strapped it on. Best of all was our maneuverability. It's called translation—technically defined as changing the spatial coordinates without rotation. I could translate up and down, right and left, forward and backward, just as they do in the movie *Star Wars*.

No doubt about it, the Gemini spacecraft was my favorite flying vehicle. But before I got to fly it, I was plagued by mishaps.

On the morning of October 25, 1965, Stafford and I were aboard our Gemini spacecraft awaiting confirmation from the tracking stations that the Agena was in orbit. We were scheduled to go just as the Agena completed its first spin around the world. The word never came. At launch plus fifty minutes Paul Haney, a NASA public affairs officer, announced that the station in Carnarvon, Australia, had reported it was receiving no signal. We later learned from telemetry data that the Agena blew up before reaching orbit.

So much for our fun that day. We were flying the last of the battery-operated spacecraft, and our time in orbit was limited to a day or two. The rendezvous was our specific objective in that short period. Without a target we were a spacecraft without a mission. So we descended in the elevator, doing what as a kid I used to call a fireman's dive—when someone at the swimming pool got cold feet on the high board and climbed back down the ladder. Stafford and I were discouraged. We had missed our turn in the launch sequence and it was uncertain when we'd fly.

As we regrouped, two heroes emerged—Walter Burke and John Yardley of McDonnell, chief project officers for Mercury and Gemini. Burke and Yardley proposed a salvo launching of two Gemini spacecraft. Gemini 7 was scheduled to begin a two-week mission in early December. If Gemini 6 could be sent up while Gemini 7 was still in orbit, we could rendezvous with Gemini 7 as the target vehicle. The Gemini 7 commander, Frank Borman, was as enthusiastic as I was, but he said no to attaching a docking adapter to his spacecraft. We would rendezvous but not dock, if the idea was approved.

A double Gemini flight had been suggested just months before by the Martin Company, the Titan contractor, but NASA said no. Burke and Yardley also encountered opposition. George Mueller, chief of manned space flight, and Chuck Mathews, Gemini manager, couldn't believe a turnaround of less than two weeks was feasible. Chris Kraft said in dismay to Burke and Yardley, "You're out of your minds. It can't be done." But Burke had gotten Bob Gilruth's ear, and Gilruth would cast a decisive vote as director of the Manned Spacecraft Center. Gilruth had initially agreed with Mueller and Mathews, but Burke pressed him. "Tell me what's wrong with it?" he asked, and Gilruth couldn't.

Kraft also came around, and he said so to Gilruth on the afternoon of October 26. Deke Slayton had been consulted by this time, and he sounded out Stafford and me. Of course we were raring to go. Gilruth sent a recommendation to Washington, and it was okayed by Jim Webb and his top deputies, Hugh Dryden and Robert Seamans. On October 28, at a press conference at his ranch in Texas, President Johnson announced the Gemini 6-7 rendezvous mission.

A rapid-fire double launch was a tremendous challenge. Gemini 7 would be in orbit for fourteen days, but to do the rendezvous with a little time to spare, we were scheduled to fly eight days after Borman and Jim Lovell.

Since there was only one Gemini launch pad, number 19, things got complicated. Our spacecraft occupied the pad, sitting atop the Titan II, which we referred to in letter-digit shorthand as GLV6 (Gemini launch vehicle 6). We'd hoped we could switch boosters and use GLV6 to launch Gemini 7, but GLV6 lacked the power to send the heavier Gemini 7 spacecraft into orbit. So GLV6 and our spacecraft were dismantled and removed from the pad. The Titan II was stored on nearby pad 20, which was not in use, and our spacecraft was secured in a building on Merritt Island.

The pace began to accelerate. Before the end of October GLV7 was in place on pad 19, and preparations of the Gemini 7 spacecraft were under way. But the toughest test, the race against time, was still to come. The clock would start ticking right after the launch of Gemini 7. When Guenter Wendt, the McDonnell pad leader, was shown a schedule of Gemini 6 pad activities, he said, "Oh, man, you are crazy." But Tom and I were confident. Our spacecraft had been counted down for launch and was set to go, once it was back on the pad. It goes without saying that we were ready too, trained to a tee.

Few changes in mission particulars were necessary. The Gemini 7 flight plan was altered, to put Borman and Lovell in a nearly circular orbit, making it easier for us to overtake them. And an electronic beacon had been installed on the Gemini 7 spacecraft, so that our radar could "see" her from a distance.

We kicked around the idea of an EVA, even considering having Stafford and Lovell change places. That would have been risky. As they made the transfer, they would have had to detach their life-support hoses and depend on a portable backup system. Besides, Lovell's suit was designed for comfort on a long flight, possibly hampering an EVA. Stafford was also tall for an astronaut, and we remembered how difficult it had been for Ed White to return to the spacecraft and close the hatch. We finally decided against an EVA.

Above all we wanted to avoid unnecessary problems. Our job was to do a rendezvous. I agreed with Borman's opposition to docking, which entailed fixing a doughnut-shaped collar to the Gemini 7 spacecraft. Static electricity could have caused the two spacecraft to weld together, with serious consequences, as there would be no way to break them apart. We agreed not to make contact, and we installed little lightning rods, metal "whiskers" like those on the trailing edge of aircraft wings, to bleed off any electrical charge.

We intended to fly in formation, though some doubted we could. Actually, formation flying is a piece of cake once you learn how. Sure, we'd be moving at about 18,000 m.p.h., but what difference did that make? It's relative motion that's significant, not total motion, just as it is with stunt teams like the Blue Angels. When you orbit the earth you have roughly forty-five minutes of daylight and forty-five minutes of darkness. We had lights on our spacecraft to help us stay in formation in the dark. If you can see two distinct lights, you can handle depth perception. I learned that trick as a Navy aviator who had to land on carriers at night.

I simply said to those who doubted our ability to pull off a rendezvous, "Just wait and see."

We did a little cross-briefing with Borman and Lovell but not much. It would be a historic first when two spacecraft met in orbit, but we were not impressed with ourselves. Stafford and I had a bow and arrow, and Gemini 7 was our target.

AGAIN, A FIREMAN'S DIVE
On Sunday morning, December 12, Tom and I were back in our

160

spacecraft. Gemini 7 had launched successfully, and Borman and Lovell were in the ninth day of orbital flight. The countdown went well, and at 9:54 we had engine ignition. A clock in the cockpit had been activated, and it indicated we had launched. They were getting the same reading at Mission Control and in the blockhouse. Tom and I also were hearing a radio transmission, "Three, two, one, zero, liftoff." No, no liftoff. I knew from the feeling in the seat of my pants we hadn't launched. I recalled from my Mercury mission the sensation at liftoff, and it hadn't occurred. Experience paid off.

We later learned that a malfunction detection system had sensed no upward movement, so valves had closed to prevent fuel from gushing into the booster engines. The engines shut down, but an electrical plug dropped from the base of the booster, activating a programmer that was supposed to start at liftoff.

These were tense moments. If we had lifted off so much as a foot, and then the engines had shut down, 150 tons of propellants encased in a fragile metal shell would have exploded, and Stafford and I would have been engulfed in flames. The rule book called for me to pull a D-ring beneath my couch that would have ignited an ejection rocket and sent Tom and me to safety.

In Gemini we didn't have an escape tower that separated the spacecraft from the booster, as we did in Mercury and would again in Apollo. We had ejection seats instead. Either Tom or I could have pulled a D-ring, and we would both have been rocketed to an altitude from which a parachute would carry us to an ocean landing. It would have been a rough ride due to high G forces, though we didn't know how rough, since the system hadn't been man-tested. No one cared to try it just for the experience. We might have suffered fractures and internal injuries but probably would have survived.

People were surprised when we didn't eject, including Kenneth Hecht, chief of the Gemini escape and recovery office. And in simulations since, given the same set of circumstances, the decision has always been to eject. In a simulation you are informed of an engine shutdown following a momentary liftoff, and you have no choice. The difference is I had my butt working for me. I knew we had not lifted off, so I didn't initiate the ejection sequence. "Fuel pressure is lowering," I reported to Mission Control. Pretty soon Guenter Wendt and his crew unbolted the hatch and helped us out of the cabin. Then we did a second fireman's dive, and we were damned mad.

I also knew that if we had ejected, the escape rocket would have destroyed the spacecraft and our flight would have been delayed indefinitely. That was not a factor in my decision to stay put, but it was satisfying to realize it later. We would be able to recycle the booster, launch within three days, and catch Gemini 7. But I still breathe a sigh of relief thinking about how close we came to another failure. On the evening of the abort we were going over telemetry data with Ben Hohmann of the Aerospace Corporation, which had a contract to monitor launch vehicles. Hohmann, who had been a Luftwaffe pilot in World War II, was a meticulous engineer. "Wally," he said, "I see something I don't like." From a telemetry trace he discovered that a dust cover had not been removed from a fuel manifold. It could have caused another engine shutdown, and this time I suspect I would have elected to eject.

I wondered about the launch crews and asked myself, "Are these guys beginning to goof?" They weren't, but they were showing the strain of working under intense pressure.

Even at a time of crisis there were moments of levity. Tom Stafford had his own D-ring and could have initiated ejection, but he had given me the nod and sat tight. He did announce his reaction, though. He said, "Oh shucks," according to NASA. We were being heard live over television and radio, but in delayed time, so NASA bleeped Tom's remark.

Later, in Apollo, radio transmissions were carried in real time, so the public was able to share an appreciation for the hammer-on-thumb syndrome. When Tom Stafford and Gene Cernan flew on Apollo 10, along with John Young as command module pilot, they took the lunar lander to within 50,000 feet of the moon. As they began their ascent, the lander spun out of control, and Cernan yelled, "Oh shit, what was that?"

INCHES APART, WINDOW TO WINDOW

Gemini 6 finally made it into orbit on the morning of December 15. I still remember hearing one of our press officers shouting, "Go, you mother." As we passed over the African continent, Borman and Lovell got a glimpse of our contrail. Our apogee was 160.5 miles, our perigee was 99.8 miles, while Gemini 7's circular orbit was a constant 186 miles. Toward the end of our first orbit I increased our speed a bit by a thruster burn, which extended our apogee to 168.6 miles. We were closing on Gemini 7, since we were nearer to the earth. At insertion into orbit we trailed her by 1,235 miles, and after one orbit we were behind by only 728.5 miles. The flight plan called for catching the target by the fourth orbit, and we were holding to the schedule.

As we passed the tracking station at Carnarvon, Australia, on the second orbit, I began an adjustment that would raise our perigee to 138.9 miles and further reduce the distance from Gemini 7. Over the Pacific I turned the spacecraft ninety degrees to the south and ignited the aft thrusters. By the end of the burn we were in the same plane as Gemini 7 with the gap reduced to three hundred miles. I was told by Elliot See, the astronaut who was Houston Capcom, that we should soon make radar contact with Gemini 7. We did, and at a range of 269 miles we were locked on. Over Carnarvon again I did a fifty-four-second burn, which increased our speed and put us into a circular orbit at an altitude of about 170 miles. We were now 200 miles from Gemini 7 and closing slowly.

At five hours and four minutes from launch I dimmed the cabin lights and peered out the window. "My God," I said, "there's a real bright star out there." It was Gemini 7, about sixty miles away, reflecting the rays of the sun. I made two midcourse corrections, and at five hours and fifty minutes into the flight we were less than one thousand yards from the target. I began to brake the spacecraft by firing the forward thrusters. When Gemini 6 and Gemini 7 were forty yards apart, there was no relative motion between them. Rendezvous!

As we got within a half mile of Gemini 7, I maneuvered with tender care. The light touch was critical. If I overthrusted, our orbit might change dramatically, and I'd have botched it. Then, as we moved to within one hundred feet, it was necessary to stop our velocity in relation to the velocity of Gemini 7, or we would have whizzed right on by. I had practiced the final phase of rendezvous over and over in a simulator, for I wasn't sure how difficult it would be to stop right next to the target.

It was tricky, but my practice paid off. Computer readings based on radar told us our closing velocity, and Tom was doing computations. "Go right," he'd say. "Go left. Speed up. Slow down." Stafford, whose eyes were accustomed to the light that illuminated his plotting board, looked outside just as the rendezvous was secure and shouted, "Holy cow, Schirra! You blew it!" He was looking at John Glenn's famous fireflies, frozen droplets of water reflecting daylight. He mistook them for a field of stars, and their random movement caused him to sense that the spacecraft was out of control. "Those are fireflies, Tom," I said, and we both laughed.

"Having fun?" I radioed to Gemini 7 when we were two hundred feet apart.

"Hello there," Borman replied.

"There seems to be a lot of traffic up here," I said.

"Call a policeman," Borman commented.

All four of us were overjoyed. We had done something we had spent years preparing for. We flew in formation for three revolutions of the earth, moving from a range of one hundred yards between us to just inches, window to window and nose to nose. Using what I called my "eyeball ranging system," I did an in-plane flyaround of Gemini 7, like a crew chief inspecting an aircraft. I could see icicles hanging from one side and sunlight reflected by the gold surface of the mylar heat shield. I was amazed at my ability to maneuver, controlling attitude with my right hand and translating in every direction by igniting the big thrusters with my left-hand mechanism. Tom and I took turns. We shared the attitude stick between us, and he controlled thrust with his right hand.

Tom and I couldn't switch seats. The spacecraft was so cramped we could barely squeeze into our couches, much less move about. But I'm almost ambidextrous. I write with my left hand and can throw and kick a ball from both sides, and I'm more accurate with a pool cue when I shoot left-handed. So controlling translation with my left hand was not difficult.

I pulled one of my favorite gotchas during the rendezvous, and it was destined for citation in U.S. Naval Academy history. Three of us were Annapolis graduates—Stafford, Lovell and I. Borman went to West Point before becoming an Air Force officer, so you know who was going to get it. When our windows got just inches apart at one point, I held up a "Beat Army" sign. But Borman topped me. Before my sign's message could be read to the world, Borman radioed: "Schirra's got a sign. It says 'Beat Navy.'"

Stafford, Lovell and I were honored at the Naval Academy, incidentally. It was during the 1966 football season, and Navy beat William and Mary. We each were presented with a Rolex watch. I still wear mine. And I got the game ball, which was made into a trophy. With the rendezvous completed Tom and I were ready to come home. "Really a good job, Frank and Jim," I said to Gemini 7. "We'll see you on the beach."

We had one last surprise in store, however. We had talked about it while we trained back at the cape. "You know, Tom, it's getting close to Christmas," I said. "We might have some fun with that." We were flying over the continental U.S. on our next-to-last orbit, when Stafford began his message.

"Houston, this is Gemini 6."

"Roger, Gemini 6," Capcom Elliot See responded.

"We have an object, looks like a satellite going from north to south, probably in polar orbit...Looks like he might be going to re-enter soon...You just might let me pick up that thing."

The guys in Mission Control were beside themselves as Tom continued, "I see a command module and eight smaller modules in front. The pilot of the command module is wearing a red suit." He then started ringing a bunch of little bells, and I took out a harmonica, a tiny four-hole Hohner. I had secured it in my suit by tying it to a pocket zipper with dental floss. I could play eight notes, enough for "Jingle Bells." It may not have been a virtuoso performance, but it earned me a card in the musicians' union of Orlando, Florida. I also received a tiny gold harmonica from the Italian National Union of Mouth Organists and Harmonica Musicians.

We were still in radio contact with Gemini 7, and Jim Lovell chimed in, "Yeah, Houston, we can also see the object."

"Too much, Gemini 7," commented See.

The upshot of our little prank? At a dinner in Washington in February 1966, where President Johnson was on hand to congratulate us, my mother sat at a table with Jim Webb, the NASA administrator. She turned to Webb and remarked, "Wasn't it nice of the boys to remind the children of the world that Santa Claus is still there?"

The bells had been a present to Tom and me from Frances Slaughter of the flight crew operations office at the cape. She had tied them to our shoes, which we customarily left outside the entrance to a spacecraft simulator. I had been given the harmonica by Mickey Kapp, a friend of Bill Dana's and the producer of the record album, *Jose Jimenez in Orbit*. Kapp also provided tapes of songs that were piped to us from Mission Control. One was "Hello Dolly," dubbed over by Louis Armstrong with the name changed from Dolly to Wally. I still have the tape. It's one of my most treasured possessions.

READY FOR THE LUNAR MISSION

As we prepared to return to earth, I thought we were really showing our stuff in Gemini. Gemini 4 demonstrated we could do an EVA. We had done the long tests, eight days in Gemini 5, fourteen days in Gemini 7. The rendezvous had exceeded expectation. Now I was about to demonstrate the first computer controlled re-entry.

In Gemini I reached the high point of my career as an astronaut. The Gemini 6 mission was the ultimate experience of my twenty-one-year flying career.

The key to a controlled re-entry was our ability to affect lift by rotating the spacecraft. Lift became a factor of rotation because the spacecraft's center of gravity was off center. By banking left or right, we would decrease range, since the spacecraft got the most lift flying straight ahead. We could fly left or right and decrease range. But it's not like looking at a runway and dropping down for a landing. Nor could we do it intuitively. We had to have a computer present us with accurate data.

A controlled lifting re-entry would assume new significance in a lunar mission, for crew survival would depend on its success. On its return from the moon an Apollo spacecraft must enter the earth's atmosphere at a precise angle. If the angle is too steep, the spacecraft will dig in and burn up. If the angle isn't steep enough, the spacecraft will bounce into a solar orbit. Either way, it's a very bad day.

Imagine that coming back from the moon is like a long cue shot, from one end of a pool table to the other. What you must do is put the ball in the far pocket. That is a tough shot, and you wouldn't like your life depending on it. But if you could stroke the ball as it rolled once or twice with your finger, the odds would be in your favor. In space terminology those strokes to alter the spacecraft's course are mid-course corrections.

We would make those corrections on return trips from the moon, and we practiced them in Gemini landings. We relied on the computer for the amount of change, and often it was just a slight touch. The computer also instructed us on the direction of change. The computer gave us constant readings on what our vector ought to be, the arrow that represents velocity and direction.

166

In Apollo we would be using an inertial guidance system, with the computer sensing changes in velocity. The vector then would be all the more important. It would be a free vector in space, just suspended out there. So long as we used time as a variable, the vector would tell us where we were headed and when we would arrive. Time becomes a very important variable when velocity keeps changing. The vector is affected by the relative position of the earth and the moon, even the sun, since the sun's gravitational field alters the motion of a vehicle en route to the moon.

There is no way a human brain could keep track of vector information. In order to progress from Mercury to Gemini and then to Apollo, we had to have access to the world of computers. Computer development was the most significant technological event of our ten-year endeavor to land a man on the moon.

FADING INTO HISTORY

Gemini 6's landing and recovery in the Atlantic Ocean, southeast of Cape Canaveral on December 16, 1965, went without a hitch. We switched off the computer at 80,000 feet, deployed the drogue parachute at 45,000 feet, and popped the main chute at 10,500 feet. We descended within range of TV cameras aboard the main recovery vessel, the aircraft carrier *Wasp* , so our return was beamed live via satellite to television audiences around the world. It was another first for Gemini 6.

Splashdown was only eight miles off the mark. As I had in Mercury, I elected to remain aboard the spacecraft, while it was lifted onto the carrier deck. The sixteen-orbit mission had spanned 25 hours, 15 minutes, 58 seconds.

Gemini 7 landed two days later. Borman and I had made a wager on who would come closer to the planned impact point, and he won by just a mile. However, I'd briefed Frank on the procedures I'd followed on the computer, and he admitted he'd been happy to have my guidance. I was pleased that both Gemini 6 and Gemini 7 had made spot-on landings. There had been computer problems on the first three Gemini flights. We had finally used the new technology to its fullest advantage.

The four of us had a grand reunion at the crew quarters at Cape Canaveral, and then there were the debriefings—scientific debriefings, engineering debriefings, and so on. They seemed endless, but I didn't object to being given an opportunity to savor the experience of a lifetime. I really felt that way about the rendezvous. On a flight from Bermuda to the cape the day after we landed in the Atlantic, I was reading newspaper reports of the mission. A writer for *National Geographic,* Ken Weaver, noticed I was frowning and wondered why. "I'm real sorry they made the rendezvous sound so easy," I said. "It may have looked easy, but only because we had practiced so much."

There was one debriefing that was great fun. Jocelyn Gill, a NASA astronomer, was in charge of an experiment that involved taking photographs of the heavens. Dr. Gill was particularly interested in something the scientists call the dim light phenomenon. For this experiment she had supplied me with very fast film, ASA 4,000, which was loaded into my Hasselblad camera. So I decided that here was a chance to settle the question of the fireflies once and for all.

I knew the fireflies were frozen molecules of vapor vented from the spacecraft, and they were with us constantly in the form of a fuzzy cloud. We could distinguish them from each other, since they reflected the different colors of the spectrum from the sun's rays. They appeared to John Glenn as fireflies. To others taking a quick look, as Tom Stafford did at the moment of rendezvous, they resembled a star field. As I said before, their source was water released in the heat exchange process that cooled our space suits. Another source was urine. "We peed all over the world," I'm fond of saying, despite the groans that come from the audience.

After the rendezvous, when we had some spare time, Tom and I snapped color photographs of the molecular cloud, one every forty five minutes. We logged each shot with a label—urine drops at sunrise, urine drops at sunset, etc. When the photos were processed at the cape, they were beautiful, and I ordered a set of prints. I had them on the table during an astronomy debriefing, mixed with other celestial photos. Dr. Gill noticed one and asked, "Wally, what constellation is this?" "Jocelyn," I replied, "that's the constellation Urion."

We took astronomy very seriously, of course. Celestial navigators use the heavens as a road map, and since the early days of Mercury we'd been students of the ancient science. On my Mercury mission one of my assignments was to observe the planet Mercury, which is not visible from earth due to its apparent proximity to the sun. I tracked Mercury through the colors of the spectrum, and with the help of an artist I produced a rendering of my observations.

Stafford and I had an astronomy assignment on Gemini 6, one that called for scientific analysis that might settle a debate once and for all. We were to search for stars of varying magnitudes through the window of the spacecraft and note those we were able to see. As had happened on my Mercury mission, our efforts to study celestial bodies called attention to a potentially serious problem. The view was hampered by a film, accumulated deposits of material, on the window.

At a debriefing in March 1963 at NASA headquarters I said the window clouding had been caused by the blast of the rocket that jettisoned the escape tower. Since there would be no escape tower on the Gemini spacecraft, I reasoned, we would not encounter the problem. "Now on Apollo," I said, "we are plus or minus on whether we can afford the weight of having window covers, but...it does have an escape rocket."

I was wrong about Gemini. Our window did film over, hindering our vision. I suspected it had been caused by the blast of the Titan II second-stage engine, though there were other possibilities. It might have been outgasing, for one—a chemical reaction of the window-pane sealant to extreme heat. At any rate we did cover the windows of the Apollo spacecraft—with shades that were removed by the departing escape tower—and the problem was solved.

Our astronomy mentor was Tony Genzano, the director of the Moorhead Planetarium in Chapel Hill, North Carolina. Tony had a great sense of humor, and he and Gus Grissom cooked up a wonderful con as we prepared for the first Apollo mission. Gus was in command of that mission. He and his crewmates, Ed White and Roger Chaffee, were at the North American plant in Downey, California, where their spacecraft was being readied. To practice their astronomical observations, they went to the planetarium at Griffith Park in Los Angeles.

For inertial guidance navigation it was necessary to designate thirty-seven named stars—Sirius, Polaris, etc.—in the celestial sphere. And it was up to us to select guide stars, to indicate the way to the named stars. With Genzano as a co-conspirator Gus submitted the names of three guide stars to the Griffith Park director—Navi, Regor and Dnoces. I was at the time assigned to command the second Apollo mission, and when my crew and I got to Los Angeles planetaruim, those names were firmly established. No one there realized they had been concocted or how. Navi is Ivan spelled backward, as in Virgil Ivan Grissom. Regor is Roger reversed. Dnoces is a backward spelling of "second," as in Edward H. White II.

With the completion of the Gemini 6 and Gemni 7 missions we had met the program objectives. From there on we would perfect techniques, the rendezvous in particular. On all five of the missions in 1966 we rendezvoused with an Agena and docked as planned. A problem developed on the first of those missions, Gemini 8, and it led to a landing far off course. But all in all Gemini was a success, a totally satisfying experience. Gemini would fade into history as we went to the moon in Apollo—the price of success.

ASIAN EMISSARIES

We went to Washington for the customary celebration, and that was when President Johnson asked Frank Borman and me to make a good-will tour of Asia. We would fly with our wives and a small entourage to Japan, South Korea, Taiwan, Malaysia, Thailand, the Philippines, Australia and New Zealand. War in southeast Asia was a source of growing concern, and the president no doubt knew that relations with countries in the region could use some shoring up.

We were to leave on February 21 aboard a KC135 cargo jet, made comfortable for passenger travel and called Air Force 1. (Several such aircraft may be designated Air Force 1, I learned, when the president isn't using his aircraft.) Our party would be made up of Frank and Susan Borman, Jo and me, a doctor, a NASA public relations type, and a protocol officer from the State Department. Notably absent were Tom Stafford and Jim Lovell. We had worked together as a team for a long time, but Tom and Jim were not asked to come along. I felt as bad as they did, but who was going to argue with LBJ?

We went to Tokyo on the first leg of a thirty-day marathon. After flying for twelve or thirteen hours, bang!—a press conference. That's the way we were used and abused over the entire trip. There were days when we made seven or eight appearances. When asked years later how I had learned to give a speech, I would say I had taken a one-month crash course in the Far East.

In Tokyo we met with Eisako Sato, the prime minister, accompanied by Edwin O. Reischauer, U.S. ambassador to Japan. We also conferred with Japanese space scientists, in keeping with the stated purpose of our tour: "To demonstrate the scientific, technological, and educational values of the U.S. space program."

On February 26 we arrived in Seoul, capital of South Korea. Hundreds of thousands of people greeted us. Borman had never been to Korea and was awed by the welcome. "My God, look at all these people," said Frank. "Aren't you glad they're friendly?" He expressed my feelings exactly.

We also visited the president of Korea, Park Chung Hee. Park had come to power five years earlier via an army coup and was sort of on probation as a free-world leader. I remember being nervous as we arrived at the presidential palace, but I can recall little else about the meeting because of an accident. As we were getting out of the car, Brian Duff, the NASA public relations man, slammed a door on my hand, lacerating the tip of a finger. Fortunately it was my left hand, so I could greet people with my right. It was also lucky that we had a doctor along, Duane Catterson, a NASA M.D. He bandaged my finger, and I got through the audience with President Park, but it was an ordeal.

Everywhere we went we were greeted by heads of state—Chiang Kai-shek in Taiwan, Ferdinand Marcos in the Philippines. They may not have been renowned democrats, but they were United States allies, and they treated us as friends. Chiang Kai-shek asked about a jade ring I was wearing, and I said my mother had bought it in Shanghai. He seemed to be impressed, and he presented me with the wings of a Chinese Air Force pilot. Frank had served with the U.S. Air Force in the Philippines, and he and Marcos got along very well. Marcos was overjoyed when Frank wore a traditional Filipino shirt.

There was a little time for laughs, but not much. Our aircraft was a flying four-star restaurant, so we had much of our fun while hopping from capital to capital. We had a diplomat on board one morning, an embassy official who was briefing us on our next stop in God knows where. He noticed that Borman was dipping a strawberry in a glass of champagne.

The diplomat remarked, "Strawberries and champagne for breakfast?"

Borman just grinned. "Doesn't everyone?"

The image of Frank Borman as a stiff-backed Army officer was immediately erased from my mind.

Perth was our first stop in Australia on March 7. I visited the NASA tracking station at the outback town of Carnarvon, five hundred miles north of Perth. I had been assigned to the station during a Mercury mission, the flight of a chimpanzee named Enos in November 1961. So I had a number of friends in Perth, among them the mayor. We all had many a pleasant evening over glasses of Swan lager beer, but on this trip formalities prevailed. The mayor greeted us wearing black robes and a white wig.

"How nice it is to be back in Perth," I said at an airport ceremony. And in an effort to be gracious I added, "If I do not find a good place to retire in the United States, I will seriously consider retiring in Perth." Leave it to the Australian press. Schirra to Retire in Perth, the headline read.

At each city in Australia stunning Rolls Royce convertibles were rolled out for us to ride in. They were plum-colored, had pigskin seats, and were equipped with a silver railing for us to grasp as we stood for ovations. Finally, Brian Duff asked how many of these fabulous automobiles the government owned. The answer was just one, which was air-lifted from city to city. It had been custom-built in Great Britain for a visit to Australia by Queen Elizabeth. When we got to Woomera, however, there was no Rolls Royce. Instead, we rode in the back of a truck.

We had received some bad news when we departed Taipei on March 1. Elliot See and Charlie Bassett, who were scheduled to fly in Gemini 9 in June, were killed in the crash of a T38 while attempting to land at Lambert Field in St. Louis. See and Bassett had flown up from Houston, accompanied in another T38 by Tom Stafford and Gene Cernan, the Gemini 9 backup crew. The four of them were headed for the McDonnell plant to get in some practice time on the rendezvous simulator. As they approached the field in bad weather and low visibility, they both overshot the runway. Stafford followed prescribed procedure. He climbed straight into the fog, circled, and landed safely. But See tried to keep the field in sight, banking left below the clouds. He was too low, and his aircraft hit the roof of a building. It happened to be a building in which McDonnell technicians were working on the Gemini 9 spacecraft.

TO OKINAWA IN AN EMERGENCY

Following a two-day visit to New Zealand and a refueling stop in the Fiji Islands, we ended our tour on March 16 in Honolulu, staying in the presidential suite of the Royal Hawaiian Hotel. This was to be our reward, for being good sports about the pace of the trip and the repeated demands for public appearances. Hawaii was a U.S. port of entry, which presented a slight problem, since we had collected a lot of loot. It was in the form of gifts from our official hosts, so we'd had no choice but to accept it. It consisted of Japanese silks and vases, pieces of Chinese sculpture, priceless items such as that. After some finagling we got it through customs.

I was ready to relax on a glorious Hawaiian beach. I had jumped into a bathing suit and was headed for a quick dip, thinking the damn rat race was worth it, we were in Hawaii. It was a favorite spot for me, the landfall of my Mercury mission, and where my mother and father retired to before moving to San Diego.

However, before I could get my feet wet I heard my name being called. I was wanted on the phone. A rear admiral told me I was to fly to Okinawa and pick up Neil Armstrong and Dave Scott.

I had followed the launching of Gemini 8 and knew that Armstrong and Scott had safely reached orbit. I did not know, because it had just occurred, that their spacecraft had spun up in a docking maneuver with an Agena. At the time we blamed the Agena for the violent motion that caused Gemini 8 to veer sharply off course and make an emergency landing in the western Pacific. As it turned out, the source of the trouble was a spacecraft thruster that would not close.

I talked to Deke Slayton by telephone. "It's your ball, Wally," he said. "Keep them under control, and bring them back to Tripler." Tripler is an Army hospital in Hawaii. Our job was to protect Armstrong and Scott. We were to prevent people from washing out their minds and diluting information they had to report. A debriefing team would be awaiting our arrival in Hawaii.

Frank Borman stayed in Hawaii to keep our wives company and protect our loot, and I flew to Okinawa with Dr. Catterson and John Fasalino, the State Department protocol officer. It was actually a sound decision to send me out there. As a former crew commander, I understood the situation as well as anyone, and I had an ideal support team. Dr. Catterson could attend to medical problems of the crew, and Fasalino could handle the press, which meant keeping reporters at a distance. John was a hefty ex-Marine, a big moose, and he would run interference for Neil, Dave and me.

On arriving in Okinawa we went immediately to Buckner Bay. There wasn't much time to reminisce, but I did remember coming to the base when I reported to the fleet as an ensign in 1945. Armstrong and Scott were aboard the destroyer *Leonard F. Mason*, which was due to dock momentarily. I was in civvies, as usual, and I stood off to the side trying not to be noticed. When I looked around, I saw more admirals and generals than I'd ever seen in one place. Then I watched a bus drive up and unload an Army band. I took Fasalino aside and said, "John, you are going to have to bulldoze the brass when our guys come down the gangway." "Roger," he replied.

As the destroyer approached the dock, Neil and Dave were on the bridge, waving at the crowd. The band played the usual oom-pah-pah. The ship evidently was low on fuel and high in the water, since she had been moving at flank speed from five hundred miles away. As she was about to put a line over the side, she glided right on by the dock. There wasn't enough fuel to reverse the engines rapidly to stop her. The skipper must have been dying a slow death, I thought, and I noticed that as the bandsmen lost their zest, the oom-pah-pahs became fainter and slower. On another unsuccessful pass by the destroyer I overheard a crusty three-star admiral standing nearby. "If she doesn't make it this time," he vowed, "I'll get a gun and sink her."

Mason finally did dock. I spirited Neil and Dave into an awaiting helicopter, took them to our airplane, and we were on our way to Hawaii. Jo had gone on to Houston with Frank and Susan Borman and our loot. I followed. So much for our vacation.

AL'S ANNIVERSARY

I was promoted to captain after my Gemini flight, but Al Shepard still outranked me and would retire as a rear admiral. However, we downplayed military status and never let it prevent us from giving each other a good ribbing. The fifth anniversary of Al's Mercury flight, May 5, 1966, was coming up as I returned to Houston, and it was an irresistible gotcha opportunity.

There was a dinner for Al, of course. All of the top officials of manned space were there—Bob Gilruth, Max Faget, Chris Kraft,

Wernher von Braun—and I was the MC. We began with a movie. Don Weiss, a civilian contractor who ran a motion picture lab for NASA, was a friend, and he put it together. There is Shepard after his flight aboard the carrier *Lake Champlain,* walking around his spacecraft and looking like a hero. And then a title flashes on the screen: *How to Succeed in Business Without Really Flying Very Much.*

At the close of the film the theme is American heroes—George Washington, Abraham Lincoln, Albert Einstein. When we get to Shepard, a voice says, "Every great man is led by another great man. Behind this great man, Alan Shepard, was none other than Captain Wally Schirra." I appear, wearing a white wig. By this time everyone is laughing. What I didn't realize was the filmmaker was in cahoots with Al. The voice continued. "Wait a minute, Wally. There's more." Then Shepard, also wearing a white wig and seated at his desk, appears on the screen. "I will see you at eight o'clock tomorrow, Schirra," he says with the authority of assistant chief astronaut, which he was at the time. "And that's an order."

I got Shepard in the end, though. When it appeared that it was time for him to speak, I had one of our press officers, a burly fellow named Ben James, stuff Al back in his chair and hold him there. Finally, I said, "Now it really is time for Al Shepard to make a few remarks." As he strolled casually to the podium, everyone got up and left the room, and Al was left with a dead microphone. We did return, though, for Al's inimitable presentation, and he scored a few gotchas.

9

Apollo: Tragedy, then Triumph

In July 1960, NASA announced a mission to the moon called Apollo while we were still training for the first Mercury flight. Intended originally just to orbit the moon, a landing on the lunar surface became, as President Kennedy said, the country's objective.

The attention of the seven astronauts and engineers with day-to-day responsibilities in Project Mercury was on our immediate flight activity. Immersed in the Mercury-Redstone missions of Al Shepard and Gus Grissom, we paid little notice to events in Washington. We may have known about a trip to Washington in June 1961 by the manager of the Space Task Group, Dr. Gilruth, but its significance only dawned on us later.

Gilruth met with Abe Silverstein, the director of Space Flight Programs at NASA headquarters, to define the moon mission. (Silverstein had named the lunar program for Apollo, the Olympian god who rode his chariot across the sun.) Gilruth and Silverstein reached a crucial decision: to proceed with all systems concurrently—a spacecraft with both a command component and

177

an orbital propulsion component, a lunar lander, boosters, launch facilities and a communications and tracking network. They also agreed that a contract for development of the spacecraft should be negotiated at once.

On July 28, 1961, Robert C. Seamans, associate administrator of NASA, approved a spacecraft procurement plan and appointed a source evaluation board headed by Max Faget, who had designed our Mercury capsule. The Space Task Group then issued an RFP, a request for proposals, to fourteen aerospace companies.

Five companies responded—Martin, General Dynamics, North American, General Electric and McDonnell. Martin was awarded the highest overall rating by Faget's evaluation board, but North American won the contract. North American was rated second overall but first for technical qualification. Top NASA officials—Seamans, Jim Webb, the NASA administrator, and Hugh Dryden, the deputy administrator—argued that North American had more pertinent experience, specifically a NASA contract to build the X15 rocket plane.

I suspect North American got the contract because of politics. California companies hadn't got a big bite of the space program, and the North American plant was located in Downey, in Los Angeles County. Decision-making at the upper levels of government is beyond me. I never understood why the Navy insisted on going ahead with the F7U Cutlass, though I assume it had to do with Chance Vought being in Dallas. There would be anguish about the NASA contract with North American in early 1967, when a fire during a spacecraft test at Cape Canaveral killed Gus Grissom, Ed White and Roger Chaffee. After the tragedy the space agency insisted North American hire key people from Martin. North American complied to the benefit of all of us.

In December 1961 program directors and engineers of the Manned Spacecraft Center met with their counterparts at North American to develop the Apollo spacecraft. A critical issue involving the best route to the moon had to be resolved before proceeding with any of the systems. Gilruth, Faget and their MSC associates (absent the astronauts, who stayed on the sidelines) had become advocates of a lunar-orbit rendezvous approach, as opposed to an earth-orbit rendezvous or a direct flight. By June 1962 they had won over Wernher von Braun, the director of the Marshall Space Flight Center in Huntsville, Alabama. Von Braun said that lunar rendezvous "offers the highest confidence factor of successful accomplishment within this decade."

The matter may have been settled within NASA, but there were dissenting voices elsewhere. Ultimately, President Kennedy was drawn into the argument. Following his visit to the cape in mid-September, three weeks before my Mercury flight, JFK went to Huntsville, where von Braun briefed him on the lunar rendezvous mission. During the briefing the president's science advisor, Jerome Wiesner, argued in favor of an earth-orbit rendezvous and engaged in a heated argument with Jim Webb until Kennedy intervened.

There were rapid developments toward resolving the issue. On October 24 Webb wrote Weisner that a contract for a lunar lander would be awarded unless his objections were so strenuous that only the president could arbitrate. Weisner still had reservations, since going ahead with the lander would mean a commitment to a lunar rendezvous. He decided to desist, however, reluctant to go to the president in the midst of the Cuban missile crisis.

On November 7, 1962, NASA awarded a contract for construction of the lunar module to Grumman Aircraft of Bethpage, New York. (The lander was called a lunar excursion module or LEM until someone on high decided that "excursion" had a frothy ring—just as in Navy carrier days, when we went on deployments, not cruises—but we still called it the LEM.) Von Braun, meanwhile, was linning up contractors—Chrysler, Boeing, North American, Douglas and others—for the various versions of the Saturn booster, which would launch Apollo.

Directing full attention to my October 3 mission, I was unaware of all the Apollo activity. I'd venture to say that was true of all the astronauts. We wern't really there for the preliminary steps that would make a lunar voyage possible, but we knew they were neccessary if we were going to make it to the moon by the end of the decade.

On the other hand I had doubts about the program. I couldn't fathom the politics. The Manned Spacecraft Center was in Houston, so the Federal Aviation Administration put its center in Oklahoma. Senator Robert Kerr of Oklahoma was the chairman of the Senate Committe on Aeronautical and Space Sciences after Lyndon B. Johnson became the vice president, and that could be the only reason.

It was President Johnson, oddly enough, who put the problem in perspective for me. While preparing for an Apollo flight, I went with my crew—Walt Cunningham and Donn Eisele—to Michoud, Mississippi, where the Saturn boosters were assembled. We met Mr. Johnson, who was visiting the facility, and chatted with him. He was certainly candid."It's too bad," said LBJ. "We have this great capability, but instead of taking advantage of it, we'll probably just piss it away."

He was right, I'm sorry to say. The Apollo hardware was junked. Not a single piece was salvaged for future use. I supported the lunar rendezvous at the time. But today, with the help of twenty-twenty hindsight, I think we'd be better off if we had gone to the moon from an earth-orbit rendezvous. It would have been more costly, and we might not have made the lunar landing in 1969, but there would be a monster space station up there today.

SHUFFLING THE CREWS

Grissom and I were assigned to command the first two Apollo missions. They were to be earth orbital flights, launched by the Saturn 1B, a scaled-down version of the big booster, the Saturn 5, which would loft later missions to the moon. And they were to be flown in a block one spacecraft, a trial model. A block one spacecraft was not equipped to dock, nor did it have a pressurized tunnel through which the crew could transfer to the lunar lander, the LEM. Also, we wouldn't carry the LEM, since it wasn't ready for flight testing.

The Saturn 1B is a big booster, a big maumoo we called it, though not nearly as big as the Saturn 5. Its first stage is powered by a cluster of eight engines, each like the V2s von Braun built in Germany in World War II, though improved. "If you make a booster that's very powerful," von Braun once said, "I will cluster it and make it even bigger." The joke was that von Braun finally built a booster with so much thrust that at liftoff the earth moved. He was proud of the Saturn 1B. Shortly after my Mercury mission I was flying with von Braun and Jim Webb to New York to attend a dinner of the Explorers Club. Von Braun gave me an autographed picture of the Saturn 1B, though neither of us then knew I'd be flying the rocket on the first of the Apollo missions.

My crew was named originally for the second Apollo mission in mid-1966, and the assignment was announced on September 29. Cunningham was technically the pilot of the LEM, and Eisele was the command and service module pilot. We soon became known as Wally, Walt and Whatshisname. People had difficulty pronouncing Donn's name, which phonetically is Eyeselee. When Jim Webb introduced us to President Johnson on the visit to Michoud, he stumbled when he got to Donn, and then he called him Isell. From then on Donn was Whatshisname.

Our flight was to be identical to that of Grissom, White and Chaffee—ten to fourteen days in earth orbit in a block one spacecraft. I argued it made no sense to do a repeat performance, and I succeeded in getting the mission scrubbed. I also got my crew eliminated from the early rotation. I had hoped to have us assigned to the first block two flight, but it went to Jim McDivitt, Dave Scott and Rusty Schweikart. We replaced the McDivitt crew as backup to the Grissom crew, and the third Apollo mission, the first to be launched by a Saturn 5, was given to a crew commanded by Frank Borman.

A lot happened between 1966 and 1968, and I'll come back to that. It's worth noting that the Borman mission was the first to go to the moon. It was a bold idea, and Webb was at first shocked by its audacity. It was only the second of the Apollo series, coming two months after mine. George Low, a program manager in Houston, had proposed sending Apollo 8 around the moon, more for political than scientific reasons. It was an insurance flight. If we failed to land men on the moon, we could still say we'd gone there before 1970.

Crews were being shuffled to the point where we joked about a lunar lottery. Deke Slayton had asked Jim McDivitt if he wanted to command the first flight to circle the moon, but Jim preferred to try docking with the LEM in earth orbit for which his crew had trained extensively. Then there were last-minute switches in Borman's crew. Tom Stafford was replaced by Bill Anders and named to command Apollo 10, the first mission to test the LEM in lunar orbit. And when Mike Collins dropped out to have surgery on his spine, Jim Lovell stepped in. Collins was reassigned to Apollo 11, the first moon-landing mission.

THE FIRE ON PAD 34

It was a comedown to be backing up Gus again, a real ego-douser. Nothing personal, for Gus and I were the best of friends and next-door neighbors. But it was like Gemini over again, with Gus in the prime slot and me as the substitute. I'd hear people imply that I had been picked for Mercury, not Apollo, and I saw some logic in that. But if I was a has-been, a seat-of-the-pants flier in an age of new technology, it applied to Gus as well—and Al Shepard and Deke Slayton. None of us was ready to admit we were finished.

So we got down to business, and we had plenty to do. Development of Gus's spacecraft—we referred to it by its number, 012—was presenting problems. Sam Phillips, the Apollo program director at NASA headquarters, spent several months in mid-1966 inspecting North American operations in California. He discovered that the company was not meeting the spacecraft manufacturing schedule, largely because subcontractors were late in making hardware deliveries. AiResearch, the maker of the environmental control system, was singled out for an especially poor performance, and Lee Atwood, president of North American, admitted in October that the launching of the first Apollo flight—it had been set for February 21, 1967—was subject to delays.

We had tackled the problem with our usual intensity—you might say we gang-tackled it, since there were six of us. We found ourselves building the command and service module piece by piece, testing as we went. We established a crew quarters at the North American plant in Downey and would fly out there on a moment's notice. When we landed in a T38 at the Los Angeles airport, a helicopter would be there to take us to the plant. There was no time to lose.

But for all our patience and effort the spacecraft was not checking out. It just didn't have the ring of a pure bell. Finally, in exasperation, Gus hung a lemon on it—literally, a big California lemon.

Spacecraft 012 was shipped to Cape Canaveral in August 1966. It was still in pieces, but the decision had been made to assemble it on the pad—pad 34, more properly launch complex 34. So for the rest of the year we commuted to Florida, flying to Patrick Air Force Base and living in the crew quarters at the John F. Kennedy Space Center on Merritt Island. (The spaceport had been named for President Kennedy following his assassination in 1963.) When Gus and I tallied our travel time for calendar year 1966, it came to 280-plus days.

On January 26, 1967, Cunningham, Eisele and I did a full-up system test of Apollo-Saturn 204, the spacecraft and the Saturn 1B booster. Full-up means we were fully powered, though we did not have the cabin pressurized with oxygen and were breathing ambient air. With about a month to go before launch we were pushing ahead, saying we were going to make this machine work. This sort of attitude is not in line with test pilot training, but we were trying to stay on schedule. It was as if we were riding a locomotive down a track with ten more locomotives bearing down behind.

After the test we held a debriefing in the ready room of the crew quarters—just Gus, Joe Shea, the MSC program manager, and I. I put it bluntly. "Frankly, Gus, I don't like it. You're going to be in there with full oxygen tomorrow, and if you have the same feeling I do, I suggest you get out."

The following day, January 27, Cunningham, Eisele and I flew back to Houston. We were aboard our T38s when Grissom, White and Chaffee were winding up a test that had lasted all afternoon. The sea-level atmosphere in the cabin had been replaced by pure oxygen at a pressure of 16.7 pounds per square inch. At 6:31 P.M. there was a cry over the radio from inside the spacecraft:

"There's a fire in here."

I heard when we landed at Ellington Air Force base. Joe Algranti, who ran our aircraft operations office, came running out. I knew something was wrong from the way Joe looked. "The Apollo crew," he said. "They burned to death."

I thought about Ed White, an Air Force lieutenant colonel who had made the first "spacewalk," and about Roger Chaffee, a Navy lieutenant commander due to go on his first mission. But mostly I though about Gus. He was one of our original seven good buddies, my next-door neighbor. I was the executor of his estate. Jo, I learned, had walked over and told Betty Grissom. She had gone by way of a hole in the fence that was there so our wives could visit each other without reporters knowing.

As test pilots must be, we are accustomed to death. The loss of a colleague, often a good friend, is not an uncommon occurrence. It doesn't mean we don't feel deeply about our friends and don't mourn their passing. When I go sailing and see the hills surrounding San Diego, I think about Shannon McCrary, the squadron skipper who is buried in a cemetery at Point Loma. He was killed while making an instrument approach, and we went to his funeral and wore a black arm band. But we don't wear a black arm band forever. We mourn the man for a little while, then we live with his loss.

Astronauts in addition to Grissom, White and Chaffee have been killed in airplane accidents, not in space activity. There was that crash in St. Louis in February 1966 that killed Elliot See and Charlie Bassett. Ted Freeman, one of the group picked for Apollo in 1963, died when his T38 collided with a flock of geese during a landing at Ellington Air Force Base. And after the Apollo accident, in October 1967, C. C. Williams, a Marine pilot, was lost after taking off in a T38 from Patrick Air Force Base.

There's a film that was made for test pilots called *You've Got to Expect Losses.* It shows a series of accidents, beginning with early attempts by man to fly, with disastrous results. More to the point, you see a Navy fighter going off the bow of a carrier, paalunk, into the sea. And there's an accident made famous by the film—of an F100 in a full stall with flames billowing from both ends of the fuselage before it blows up. Ghoulish as it might sound, we laugh when we watch that film.

When I say we don't wear a black arm band forever, I do not mean we are not affected by the loss of a friend. I do mean that we expect losses, and we learn to live with them. In January 1967 the NASA people didn't know how to live with losses. The fire really got to them. It was weeks later that I took Bob Gilruth for a sail on my Cal 25. Bob was at the tiller and he just fell asleep. Maybe it was the first chance he'd had to relax, to realize he had to push ahead and forget the tragedy. Gilruth was carrying a tremendous load. He had been like a father to us, though he was not that much older.

Certainly, an individual has a right to his own approach to death. Gus and I were different in this. He thought about death, talked about "busting his ass," and had mementos he wanted to pass around in case he died. Perhaps he anticipated disaster and needed to express it.

If anything I'm more of a fatalist than Gus was. I don't talk about death. I never think about it. It's just not something I'm involved with. I've learned to train out fear. It's important to do this. It's a creed with me. On that Gemini flight, when we had the hold at liftoff, I was apprehensive, but I wasn't afraid. Why? Because I was in control of the situation. When I talk about training out fear I mean training to the point that there are no surprises. We used to joke about it, and the best story involved a numbskull, the brother of the gorgeous wife of an ambitious Hollywood producer. The producer wants the idiot out of town, so he finds a walk-on part for

him in a New York production of the *1812 Overture*. All the guy
has to do is speak one line. "Hark to the cannon's roar." By the time
he lands in New York, he's got the line down cold, "Hark to the
cannon's roar." He rushes to the theater, puts on a costume, and
as he appears on stage, there is the roar of the cannon. The guy says,
"What the fuck was that?"

An investigation of the fire was conducted by a NASA review
board. Its chairman was Floyd Thompson, the director of Langley
Research Center, and among its members were Max Faget, the chief
of engineering and development at MSC in Houston, and astronaut
Frank Borman. The source of an electrical spark that might have
caused the fire was traced to an area the size of a grapefruit beneath
Gus's left foot. But the real danger discovered by the board was
the pure oxygen atmosphere of the cabin. This condition, coupled
with a hatch that opened inward and was sealed shut, caused death
by suffocation.

Lee Atwood, the president of North American, remained concerned about the fire long after he retired. In 1987 he sent me an
analysis in which he expressed his regret. "If the question had been
properly put," he wrote, "...that is, did you know that the astronauts
are being locked in with all that electrical machinery, and the
spacecraft is being inflated to 16.7 pounds per square inch with
pure oxygen? I believe a whistle would have been blown."

Remedial action was taken to prevent recurrences. All flammable
materials were removed from the spacecraft, and a hatch was
designed to open out—it was also equipped with explosive bolts—as
it had on the Mercury and Gemini spacecraft. And according to a
formula devised by Faget, the cabin would be pressurized before
launch with a mixture of 60 percent oxygen and 40 percent nitrogen,
which was considered safe and was acceptable to the medical team.

We had finally lost our bet on pure oxygen and that surprised
us. We thought by this time it was pretty safe. We had used pure
oxygen in Mercury and Gemini without an incident. We theorized
that the stuck thruster on Gemini 8 was caused by a short circuit,
but there was no fire. Perhaps we lucked out.

In the zero gravity of space, when a fire starts, there is no air to
support it, so it immediately burns out. At sea level, as we were
sadly reminded on January 27, 1966, convection currents feed the

fire. There aren't many substances that don't burn in pure oxygen. On future flights we would continue to use pure oxygen in space, replenishing the system with oxygen as the nitrogen leaked out. We realized we would still be breathing oxygen during re-entry, and a fire would then take all the fun out of the mission. But by then the spacecraft would be thoroughly checked out, so the danger would be minimal.

Some heads rolled in the aftermath of the tragedy. The Apollo mission director of the NASA headquarters, Everett Christiansen, resigned, and George Low replaced Joe Shea as the program manager at MSC in Houston. At NASA's request Atwood hired William Bergen to take over from Harrison Storms as president of North American's Space and Information Systems Division. Bergen came from the Martin company.

Bergen brought along two Martin engineers, assigned them to key Apollo positions. John Patrick Healey became the manager of spacecraft development at Downey—specifically, Healey was in charge of factory preparations of the first block two spacecraft, command and service module (CSM) 101. Bastian Hello—he was nicknamed Buzz, which seemed appropriate for someone named Hello—was the boss of North American's operations at Cape Canaveral. (Buzz retired recently, replaced as the Washington representative of Rockwell International by former astronaut Jim McDivitt.)

Whether or not it was related to the problems of the space program, this was a period of instability in the contractor world, and we felt the effect of corporate realignment and executive shakeups. In September 1967 North American merged with Rockwell-Standard to become North American Rockwell. And in April 1969 McDonnell Aircraft and Douglas Aircraft became McDonnell Douglas. Douglas was the manufacturer of the Saturn S4B stage. McDonnell, while it had been the spacecraft builder in Mercury and Gemini, did not have a major Apollo contract.

Many of the company engineers and project officers became close friends. It was bound to happen, given the teamwork that was required over long periods. Take John Healey, who is retired now from North American. I get a call from John Patrick on every anniversay of the Apollo flight, and he says, "Thank you, Wally, for compromising at the right time and being hard-nosed at the right time." That's the ultimate compliment for a test pilot. Another example is Harrison Storms, who left North American under a cloud. We kept in touch, and when I became the chairman of the board of an environmental company in the 1970s, I made Stormy a director. He recently asked me to join him on a company board. And there is John Yardley, the McDonnell project officer at Cape Canaveral. He was so upset by the loss of of the first Apollo crew that he suffered a nervous breakdown. He recovered, thankfully, and went on to become president of McDonnell Douglas Astronautics.

There was a congressional investigation of the fire. In April 1967 I was called to appear along with Deke Slayton, Al Shepard, Jim McDivitt and Frank Borman. It was exasperating having to hear a half-assed politician expound on the deficiencies of the Apollo program. My hat was off to Borman. As a member of the review board, he was our spokesman, and he stated our case succinctly. "We are trying to tell you," he said in response to a congressman's question, "that we are confident in our management, and in our engineering, and in ourselves. I think the question is really: Are you confident in us?" Borman then made a plea for ending the witch hunt, so we could get on with the program. I sensed that Frank had put the message across to the House subcommittee on NASA oversight, Olin Teague's subcommittee. So much for hand-wringing.

Bob Gilruth assigned Frank to take a team of MSC engineers to North American's Downey plant to oversee safety modifications of the spacecraft—an environmental system that used an oxygen-nitrogen mixture before launch, fire-resistant wiring, new plumbing, a hatch that opened out, and so on.

On May 9, 1967, Jim Webb announced the team for the first manned Apollo mission, having cancelled all flight assignments after the fire. Schirra, Cunningham and Eisele—Webb got the names right this time, but we were still known to the ground crews as Wally, Walt and Whatshisname—would be the prime crew, backed by Stafford, Young and Cernan. He also named a support crew. Jack Swigert, Ron Evans and Bill Pogue would maintain a flight data file, develop emergency procedures in the simulators, and prepare the cockpit for countdown tests. (I asked Swigert to establish procedures in the event of a fuel tank explosion in space, and just such an explosion occured on Apollo 13 in April 1970. Swigert was aboard Apollo 13, and his checklist was used to get the crew safely home.)

Our spacecraft would be CSM 101. It would be boosted by a

Saturn 1B, not a Saturn 5, so we would not achieve the velocity to escape earth orbit. We would not carry the LEM, as it wasn't ready to fly, but we would practice docking with the S4B stage of the booster, to which the LEM would be attached during launch on trips to the moon. We would remain in orbit for at least ten days, the minimum duration for a voyage to the moon and back.

Our flight was designated Apollo 7. The flight that Grissom, White and Chaffee would never make had been named Apollo 1 in their honor. Gus had pushed for an "Apollo 1" patch unsuccessfully. After the accident Betty Grissom, Pat White and Martha Chaffee stepped in and NASA agreed.

There were no Apollo 2 and 3 flights. George Low did try to apply those names retroactively to unmanned tests in 1966, but the idea was vetoed by a committee at NASA headquarters. Three unmanned tests that preceded Apollo 7 were named, however. Apollo 4, the first "all-up" test of the three-stage Saturn 5, went off on November 9, 1967. On that flight a block one spacecraft with block two modifications was put into orbit and recovered. Apollo 5, launched on January 22, 1968, was the first test of the lunar module. The LEM was sent into orbit by a Saturn 1B, the one that had been designated as the booster of AS 204, or Apollo 1. The main objectives were achieved, and the LEM was allowed to disintegrate on re-entry into the atmosphere. Apollo 6, on April 4, 1968, was a Saturn 5 test with a block one spacecraft with block two improvements, including the new hatch. The spacecraft passed its test, but the "pogo bounce" of the Saturn—the pogo effect was a resonance caused by a partial vacuum in the firing chamber of the engine—was a subject of concern. The problem was soon solved by injecting helium into the liquid oxygen system.

We were go for launch, which was scheduled for the last quarter of 1968.

THE TRAIN IS MOVING OUT

After the fire there was a complete overhaul of the block two series—an overhaul in the basic design of the spacecraft, an overhaul in our thinking. Frequently, in the early part of 1967, there were emotional meetings. They had to do with when we would fly, even though Webb hadn't yet announced that we were the crew. NASA management was pushing for us to go in January or February 1968. My guess was after April 1968.

188

To me the major milestone would be the altitude tests at Cape Canaveral. People believed the crew bought the spacecraft when it was shipped to Florida from California in May 1968. They were wrong. I said many times that we would not accept CSM 101 until it had completed its run in the altitude chamber—similar to the launch pad test where fire killed Grissom, White and Chaffee.

When the altitude tests were a success, in June 1968, I was elated. We would fly by the end of the year. "We're on a high-speed track," I chortled. "This train is moving out."

Apollo 7 was going to be my last mission. I intended to retire, and I would make it official before we flew. There were a number of reasons. For one I wanted to quit while I was ahead. I also wanted it to be clear that I was single-minded about the Apollo 7 mission, that I cared about nothing else.

I had changed over the span of time that encompassed my three flights. As the space program had matured, so had I. I was no longer the boy in scarf and goggles, the jolly Wally of space age lore. When the original crew of the first Apollo was lost, I became deeply involved in deciding where we were headed. And when I realized we would try again with me in command, I resolved that the mission would not be jeopardized by the influence of special interests— scientific, political, whatever. I was annoyed by people who did not consider the total objective of the mission. I would not be an affable fellow when it came to decisions that affected the safety of myself and my two mates.

There were those involved in launching us who never got the message—well-intentioned engineers whose enthusiasm for technological achievement often ran counter to the well-being of the crew. They and I were on a collision course, and eventually we clashed. My decision to quit made it easier to say I didn't give a damn. I wasn't so susceptible to criticism. I cared not a whit about being in the good graces of the support folks, including the hierarchy.

On September 20, 1968, I announced that I would retire from the Navy and from NASA, effective July 1, 1969.

Jim Webb's announcement of the Apollo 7 crew was delivered at a hearing of the Senate space committe. Webb sounded defensive, as if he needed to assure the senators of our dedication. The Schirra team, he declared, is on its way to the North American plant in Downey "to start a detailed, day-by-day, month-by-month association with block two spacecraft number 101."

Actually we had started our work before the investigation of the fire ended. We had learned of our flight assignments in April, and I immediately got everyone together—the prime crew, the backup crew and the support crew. We went to Miami and borrowed the house of Bill Hartack, the jockey. The purpose was to get our minds off the accident and to concentrate on what lay ahead. Hartack's house was in a resort called Miami Springs Villas, and we arranged with manager Art Bruns for three days of absolute privacy. We could telephone out through a switchboard, but we would take no calls. In that brainstorming session we fit our individual responsibilities into a schedule that extended to an Apollo 7 launch a year and a half later.

Jack Swigert of the support crew told me he had sent requests to North American and was meeting with resistance. I called Lee Atwood. I hardly knew him at the time, though we later became good friends. I laid it on the line. "Lee, roll up your sleeves and start helping us," I said, "or there will be crew resignations. And we'll not withhold our reasons for leaving."

Atwood and his people did get on board the train. Bill Bergen, who had been hired to supervise our program, had a bunk put in his office. Dale Myers, the Apollo manager—his career at North American began during World War II—also made the commitment we expected. My confidence in the spacecraft contractor was resuscitated.

There was one company man who did more than anyone to restore my faith. He was John Patrick Healey, who had come to North American with a mandate to prepare our spacecraft for a successful flight. In our first meeting Healey and I were like two bantam roosters in a pit. But instead of engaging in a mutually destructive competition, we became allies and good buddies.

I've known few engineers as adept as Healey, and I learned a lot from observing his technique. He was usually quietly persuasive, but he could become angry when it was appropriate. The engineers and technicians who reported to him knew when he was displeased, but he followed the rule I was taught at the naval academy: berate people in private, commend them in public. When he was at Martin—or Martin's, as he told me they call the company in Baltimore—he worked on Titan II, the Gemini booster. He remained in charge of the Apollo spacecraft after the merger of North

American and Rockwell. He later became vice president for manufacturing of the company's space division.

With Healey guiding the plant crews, we labored day and night getting the first spacecraft ready. We rebuilt the life support system, which was a complex task. We would breathe a mixture of oxygen and nitrogen at sea level pressure, sixteen pounds per square inch, before launch. In space we would breathe pure oxygen, but the pressure could not be greater than five pounds per square inch, or the spacecraft would explode. We also scrapped the wiring system, replacing what looked like spaghetti with flat, multicolored ribbons of wire. Incidentally, those ribbons of wire we developed—I'm careful not to say we invented them, but they were an innovation of the space program—ultimately had vast commercial use.

In early 1968, as we were finishing the Downey phase of mission preparation, I inspected the spacecraft. It was similar to a command review in the Navy, with Bergen and Healey and a few NASA honchos standing by. Dressed in the required spick-and-span white suit and headgear, I was careful upon boarding not to step on any electrical or mechanical parts, anything that might be damaged. But it was a tight fit, and my knee landed on a bunch of wires. When it did, I felt a sharp slap on my face, and I heard a woman's voice: "Don't you dare touch those wires. Don't you know we lost three men?" When she was told who I was, she felt embarrassed, but I assured her she needn't be. "Keep it up," I said. "I want people like you working on this spacecraft."

On another occasion at Downey I walked uninvited into a darkened conference room where the door was open. There were slides on the screen, pictures of the couches we would sit on or lie in during the mission. They were couches for the block one spacecraft, I knew only too well. There had been lengthy discussions about replacing them with couches that would afford greater protection for the crew in the event of a land landing. Someone suddenly turned on a light and said, "Oops, there's Wally."

"Yes, gentlemen," I said. "And when *do* we get the block two couches?"

The answer was we wouldn't get them in time for Apollo 7. So I said, "I think we ought to discuss the mission rule about winds at the cape. We will not land on land. We will land on water." Early in Apollo, in 1964, a North American engineer concluded from tests that "land impact problems are so severe that they require abandoning this mode as a primary landing mode." Despite the engineering language the point was clear: a land landing meant serious injury.

The decision had been made, of course, for an ocean landing. We had splashed down in Mercury and Gemini and had trained Apollo for a recovery at sea. So my only concern, but a major one, was the point of impact in the event of an abort during launch. Under certain wind conditions we would be blown back over Florida as we descended by parachute. I said, "Okay, we'll compromise. We'll fly with the old couches, but I want it to be a mission rule that we don't launch if the winds are unfavorable."

I was adamant and thought we had a deal. It would turn out I was wrong.

There would be no compromises when it came to fire safety. I would insist on strict observance of the precautions, although a few of them seemed to border on ludicrous. We were not allowed to take anything to read, for example—no books or magazines. Nor could we take anything made of paper to play with, such as cards or puzzles. We would find boredom a serious problem as we progressed through ten-plus days in orbit.

I did draw the line on one procedure that was suggested to reduce the risk of fire. Some mission planners wanted to shave all the hair off our bodies. I argued that the hair would grow back in the course of the mission, and the new hair would be just as flammable as what had been shaved off. I also intimated that if the danger was such that hair was a hazard, then maybe I'd rather not fly the machine after all. The powers that be relented.

I knew I had no choice but to quit smoking before the Apollo flight. To light up is to burn up in a pure oxygen atmosphere—it's as simple as that. I had been trying to quit for ten years. In Mercury and Gemini I had put my habit on hold for a day or so. So in January 1968 I began the painful process. I had been smoking OPCs (other peoples cigarettes) for a while. I put an end to that by giving everyone I'd mooched from a carton, and as I did I said to them: "Die!" It's an effective way to quit—I never smoked again—and to terminate friendships.

I had just quit smoking when I was told by those brilliant mission planners that I ought to learn to do without coffee. They had the backing of Chuck Berry, our chief medical officer. I said, "Oh, no. This is terrible. You're asking a Navy guy to give up coffee.

You're crazy.'' I battled with Gilruth, Berry and a team of psychologists for a couple of months in a series of meetings at MSC Houston. They said there was no caloric value in coffee, it was just a stimulant. And I said, "Yeah, all it does is make me happy."

I wouldn't give on this one. I had studied the fuel cell that would supply electrical power on the mission. It produced water as a by-product, and it was about 155 degrees Fahrenheit. We would have ample hot water. I had also experimented with freeze-dried coffee crystals, and I liked Maxim, the Maxwell House brand. I even had plastic bags desiged to carry the crystals. I argued that coffee added little in weight or volume to spacecraft stores.

I wasn't going to lose the coffee argument, even if it meant resorting to a ruse. I picked a meeting at the Manned Spacecraft Center when I knew all the head sheds—Bob Gilruth, Deke Slayton, Chuck Berry—would be there. (A head shed is a honcho, an official at the top of the command chain.) At the break a cart was rolled into the conference room with Danish pastry but no coffee. No coffee? I then rose and spoke. "Gentelmen, since you deem it inappropriate for the crew of Apollo 7 to drink coffee on the mission, I thought you might try doing without it for just one day."

The problem was solved to my satisfaction. And after the mission, at a meeting of the head sheds at MSC, I showed a color movie of reconstituted coffee in a clear plastic bag. Air and water don't mix easily in a weightless condition, so it showed bubbles forming random patterns, a newly discovered scientific phenomenon. I guess I got my point across.

In the spring of 1968 we took a break and went hunting for a few days on Catalina Island off the southern California coast. The trip had been arranged by Frank Compton, a North American engineer and a world-class gotcha player. My Apollo 7 team was there, along with Deke Slayton, Tom Stafford and several other astronauts. It was a serious hunt, and we managed to shoot a few goats whose forebears had been transported from the Andalusian region of Spain. It also was the subject of a home-movie classic: *The Epic Hunt at the Island of Catalina*. The film has been shown on numerous occasions, including a celebration of the twenty-fifth anniversary of Al Shepard's Mercury flight at the National Air and Space Museum in Washington.

There is a scene in the movie of the Apollo 7 crew coming out of the ocean after a less than nominal mission. I'm carrying a broken control stick, Cunningham has a toy rifle, and when Eisele empties a plastic gun cover, out flops a tuna fish. Actually Compton filmed this sequence in Palos Verdes, a beach resort near Los Angeles, and spliced it into the Catalina movie.

After the filming we went with Compton to the home of a friend of his to clean up and get warm. Frank then offered to lend us his car, a company car, to drive to Downey, while his wife Nancy took him to his office in El Segundo. As she and Frank were leaving, Nancy asked what she was supposed to do with the tuna fish. We said we'd get rid of it.

We disposed of the fish by hiding it in Compton's company car beneath the front seat. We then drove to Downey and left the car in the North American lot, forgetting that Eisele had put a starfish he had found on the beach in the trunk. When Compton picked up his car the next day, he wondered about the awful odor and thought he had discovered its source when he found the starfish in the trunk. But the following morning the smell was worse—so bad, in fact, that it made him ill on the way to work. We were back in Houston, and that afternoon I got a telegram from Frank: "Urgent. Smell. I give up. Where did you hide it?"

The spacecraft was shipped to Florida in late May 1968 aboard the Super Guppy, a ballooned-out cargo carrier that had been built by welding together two Boeing C97 Stratocruisers and equipping it with extra wide doors. The Super Guppy cruised at only 250 m.p.h., so once we did a final check of CSM 101 and kissed her good-bye, Healey and I had some time to kill. As luck would have it, we could make it to Indianapolis just in time for the 500.

I called Jim Rathmann, and he got us pit passes that enabled us to go out among the competing cars. This is my favorite Healey story because it shows him to be the consummate engineer. Just before the race we were walking on the grid where the thirty-three entries were warming up. We noticed that mechanics were working on one of them, evidently having decided to change the gear ratio at the last minute. They were pulling gears out of the rear end and replacing them. "That car won't last two laps," said Healey. I asked why, and John replied, "Because the gears haven't been nerfed." Nerfing, he explained, is rubbing sharp edges off new gears by gradual use. "Those gears will chew themselves up in about two laps," he said, "and the car will be out of the race." Healey was off by only one lap. The car dropped out after three.

I wrote in a training report for May 1968 that I had taken an engineer from North American to observe a series of two hundred very low altitude orbits.

COUNTDOWN AT THE CAPE

CSM 101 and Saturn 1B 205 were mated at launch complex 34, pad 34 to us, where the fatal fire had happened. Thinking about it kept me on my toes. I was not pleased with pad discipline, and I suggested to Buzz Hello that North American hire Guenter Wendt from McDonnell, who had been a superb pad leader. We badly needed him. Hello was a competent manager, but he lacked Healey's ability to judge people, and on that occasion he misread me completely.

"Sure, Wally," he said. "I'll get you a rubber piggy doll if you want."

"Wrong, Buzz," I answered, and if there was a steel edge to my tone, it was intended. "We made some big waves out in California, and you'd better believe we'll make them here too. We want the best people available, and we won't hesitate to name them. Wendt is the best. He did all of the Mercury and Gemini launches. He will not take any nonsense from your employees on the pad. If there is any trouble out there, he can be trusted to let us know." Guenter Wendt returned as pad leader. We then began an exhaustive series of tests on the pad.

We also practiced rendezvous in a simulator, as Tom Stafford and I had done in Gemini. On Apollo 7 we planned to turn around after launch and fly in formation with the S4B stage, which would remain in orbit with us for a couple of days. (On Saturn 5 missions the S4B would power the command and service module and the lunar module on the voyage to the moon, and it would impact on the lunar surface, having separated from the CSM and LEM.)

In the rendezvous simulator I confronted the size of the Apollo spacecraft, the command and service module combined. Compared-with the Mercury and Gemini spacecraft, it was a monster. It was like making a transition from a fighter pilot to bomber pilot, and I wasn't altogether pleased about it.

As we approached the lunar mission, in 1965-66, we had decided we needed the best simulators man could devise in an electronic age. We wanted to look out of a window and see the closest possible approximation of celestial surroundings. We were fond of saying we were finished with tinker toys.

I was asked in a high-level meeting at the Manned Spacecraft Center what I would propose as a budget for these super-duper simulators.

"What's the cost of a lunar mission?" I asked. The answer was $500 million. "Then put $500 million aside for simulation." That shook up some people, but it was an accurate estimate, and it indicated we weren't fooling.

We got our money's worth. As we looked out the windows, we could see color television pictures of the real-world exterior. We were given an earth-sky reference and could make out earth features such as rivers and mountains and clouds and celestial bodies encircling the earth. If we picked out a star, say Sirius near the constellation Orion, we could follow it from window to window, as we slowly rolled the simulated spacecraft. Simulator fidelity was such that I knew in advance of the Apollo 7 flight when certain features would come into camera range. The simulator told me precisely when five points in a row over a two hundred-mile range—my eyeball, the camera, the spacecraft widow, the S4B stage and a point on earth, which happened to be Cape Canaveral—would line up.

In August 1968 NASA decided on a launch date of October 11. We even had a flow chart time-tagging events through liftoff. The schedule seemed prophetic. We adhered to it so closely that for the last six weeks of a day-by-day countdown we knew with confidence just when we would launch.

Cunningham, Eisele and I were ready to fly with a month still to go. There were, of course, the usual last-minute changes caused by people who had a hard time believing we were really going to fly. I built a buffer of associates around me to keep these people at a distance. And we avoided their advice—well intentioned but very distracting—by ignoring them.

We called the items that took our minds off the mission funny-looking things. Once on a hunting trip in Wyoming I asked the old-timer who was guiding me to identify some peculiar stones I had collected. Those are FLRs, he said. I thought I knew a bit about geology but to my chagrin had never heard of FLRs. I admitted this to my guide, who explained, "FLRs are funny-looking rocks."

So an FLT was a funny-looking thing. It was also an unexpected event, a dreadful surprise. We would cope with a few of those on the Apollo 7 mission.

10 Apollo: Onward to the Moon

NOT THE HAPPIEST GUY IN TOWN

The prospect of a land landing because of a launch abort continued to worry me. If we wouldn't accept the risk, I was told in a meeting in Bob Gilruth's office in Houston in September, the odds on a mission in October were quite low. "Gentlemen, we are men with wings on," I said. "We are willing to take risks, if we understand the odds." I carefully reviewed the odds, and it was clear the risk would be greatly diminished by favorable winds at liftoff, winds that didn't exceed eighteen knots from a direction that would cause a land landing after an abort.

That was encouraging, but my concern wasn't going to just fade away. It had to do with eliminating surprises by training out fear, gaining confidence, relying on people. I was depending on my fellow astronauts, who were evidently overridden by overzealous honchos. "That plot was jumping all over the cape," Gene Cernan, who would take two trips to the moon, told me later.

Cernan was talking about unstable weather. I knew the winds were high, and I thought we might scrub. I was the last one who wanted to postpone the mission, but I had been adamant about the

199

rule that would prevent a land landing. My worst fears were confirmed. The winds at liftoff were between twenty and twenty-five knots. If the booster had failed in the first sixty seconds and we had used the escape tower, we'd have been blown several miles back across Florida, probably injuring us severely. A mission rule had been broken. Needless to say, I was not the happiest guy in town.

I don't accept accusations that I acted out of temperament, some dark side of my nature. I was angry, and with good reason. The mission pushed us to the wall in terms of risk. They did it again on Apollo 12, launching in a thunderstorm. As we lucked out, so did Pete Conrad, Dick Gordon and Alan Bean. But fate has a way of catching up, as it did with the space shuttle *Challenger* explosion.

BEAUTIFUL BEGINNING

It was a telling moment on each of my flights when the gantry was pulled away, and the crew was left alone in its spacecraft atop the booster. This is the moment when we lost real touch with earthlings, who became voices by radio only. It's as of this moment that the white room, in which Guenter Wendt and his crew had labored diligently, just disappeared. It was then on the morning of October 11, 1988, that Donn Eisele made a remark I'll never forget:

"I wonder where Guenter went."

There's a sense of elation when the bolts blow, to use an old-timer's term. The hold-downs release, and the big maumoo leaves the launch pad. The excitement is tremendous, sustained by the knowledge that all the effort over years of getting ready has come to a climax. We are really on our way now!

There was little for the crew to do in the early moments except monitor the dials and listen to the ground controllers. Tom Stafford, my Gemini partner, was the Capcom, and he was saying we looked good. As we passed through the abort points, I sighed with relief as far as high winds were concerned, but I was perplexed by the reneged commitment. There would soon be other issues to be argued by the crew and the men at Mission Control.

We had not had close photographic coverage of the unmanned Saturn 1B liftoffs, so I was somewhat startled by the fireworks at staging, as the Chrysler S1B first stage gave way to the Douglas S4B second stage. The S1B is a Wernher von Braun design, a cluster of eight H1 Rocketdyne engines with a total thrust of 1.6 million pounds. The S4B is fired by one J2 engine, built by North American Rocketdyne, and it produces 200,000 pounds of thrust. It was like being in an erupting volcano, with sparks and fire and smoke and debris all over the place.

We boomed right up to orbit, though, on a comfortable ride compared to Mercury and Gemini, thanks to the much bigger booster, the first built for manned flight as opposed to delivering military payloads. On a Mercury launch we sustained a force of almost ten Gs, and in Gemini it was five or six. In an Apollo launch we climbed into orbit never exceeding one G. We could perform the jobs we did in the simulator—reach up and do switches, everything but climb out of our couches. I said to myself, " Now I'm a bomber pilot."

Once in orbit we turned around, very slowly as always, to simulate the initial docking with the S4B. On lunar missions this maneuver would achieve retrieval of the LEM, which would ride to the moon on the nose of the command and service module. As we moved in on the S4B, I realized something was amiss. One of the panels of the LEM adapter section had not opened fully, which would have spelled failure, had we been playing for real. I made a note to recommend that the panels be jettisoned on future flights. They were, and Jim McDivitt, the commander of the first mission to test the lunar module, was grateful for my suggestion.

We pulled away from the S4B and sped some distance from it—one hundred miles or more. The main engine of the command and service module was, as Eisele said, "a real boot in the rear," and when I tested it for the first time, the jolt plastered us in our seats. I planned to return for the final rendezvous, but at the moment I wanted some room. These were big machines, I realized, and we couldn't zap them back and forth, up and down, as we had in Gemini. Also, we had reached the end of our first day according to clocks in Houston. "Thank God it's Friday," the government workers at the space center were saying.

My flight time line, the crew duty schedule, called for one of us to be awake at all times. And as I have repeatedly reminded people, with a grin naturally, two of us might have slept simultaneoulsy, but never together. On that first night Eisele had the watch, and Cunningham and I slid below into an area under our couches where we could be restrained from floating free. When I awoke on Saturday morning, I could hear Eisele in an argument with Mission

Control. I put on a headset and heard a ground controller say, rather insistently, that our first television transmission was on the agenda for that day.

For the first time in the space program we were equipped with an onboard TV camera and capable of transmitting to Houston coverage of our mission. With the cooperation of the networks, the first live-from-space television show would be beamed to America and the world. The live TV idea was propoganda, pure and simple, and a number of engineers had opposed it, maintaining that the camera added unnecessary weight. The astronauts remained neutral, but we'd resist anything that interfered with our main mission objectives. On this particular Saturday morning a TV program clearly interfered.

"When Wally hears about this, he's going to be pretty damned annoyed," Eisele was saying. "I am hearing about it, and I am pretty damned annoyed," I chimed in. "We're not going on television today. It's not in our time line." The time line was carefully constructed so we could perform our tasks in sequence, methodically checking out every piece of equipment. We were scheduled to test the TV circuit later that day, and we'd test it before using it. It was an electrical circuit, and I had not forgotten that an electrical short had resulted in the loss of the Apollo 1 crew.

The guys in Houston refused to take no for an answer. Deke Slayton tried to persuade me to change my mind, and I said, "Sorry, Deke. No TV today." I wouldn't budge. I had this picture in my head of the first TV show in space. We come on the screen, and I say, "Oh, hi everybody, here we are. Let's have some fun and games." And then, pooom—"Sorry, we're not here anymore."

There was another good reason for postponing our debut in the media world. In fact, prior to launch it had been confirmed that we would not go on television until we had completed the rendezvous on the second day. From our first encounter with the S4B I knew our final rendezvous would not be a piece of cake. I was not prepared for the nightmare that would take place. First, we weren't as well equipped as Tom Stafford and I had been when we made the first Gemini rendezvous. We were without radar and unable to read our range to the target and our closing velocity. And our computer was so sophisticated that it would refuse to function if slightly abused. Second, I wasn't altogether confident that this big bomber

I was piloting was capable of slowing down before we collided with the S4B.

We made it through the rendezvous, with each of us aging about a year. The braking phase was traumatic. It was difficult to sense the closing motion, though I knew we were still approaching, when all of a sudden the S4B loomed large in our path. We got to within a hundred feet of her, which was close enough for me. The S4B was spinning and tumbling like an angry whale. We pulled away, and once at a safe distance we celebrated—with a plastic bag of hot coffee.

We checked out the TV circuit, and on Sunday we premiered "The Wally, Walt and Donn Show" from, as we said, "the Apollo room high atop everything." We had a lot of fun, cruising about the cabin to demonstrate weightlessness and showing cue cards that had been printed on a special nonflammable material. The messages on the cards were old radio cliches like, "Keep the cards and letters coming, folks." Or they were local jokes using a slightly tattered theme. "Are you a turtle, Deke Slayton?" "Are you a turtle, Paul Haney?" Haney was our press officer in Houston, and it probably was his idea to turn on the TV camera early and out of sequence, which I had vetoed.

AND THREE'S THE CHARM

I'm not one who enjoys boring holes in space, or as the lady says in the song, "Flying up high with some guy in the sky is my idea of nothing to do." We were on day four when I realized that 10.8 days is an eternity. Fascinating as it may seem to anyone who hasn't flown in space, twenty-four hours is still twenty-four hours. Up there a twenty-four-hour day is punctuated by sixteen ninety-minute orbits, and on each orbit you can watch earthrise and earthset. You soon quit saying "Golly-gee."

I was wearing a watchband made of Velcro, the hard-stick material. To it I had attached a small metal calendar for October 1968, and as each day passed, I scratched it off. It was as if I was a prisoner or a man marooned on an island. As we reached October 15, almost the midway point, I became agonizingly aware that we had over six days still to go. Boredom was getting to me.

I noticed after the flight that I had forgotten to cross off October 21, our last full day in space. It's interesting that I didn't keep book on the final day. I was becoming acclimated to the mission. I was even enjoying it. But I didn't change my mind about another flight. I was glad I had decided to quit while I was ahead. I said in Gemini, when we made three attempts to fly, that three's the charm. The same may be said for for my career as an astronaut. A Mercury, a Gemini and an Apollo add up to three. And they were charming.

We played space games in an effort to beat the boredom. Walt Cunningham would make a ring with his thumb and forefinger, and I would try to shoot a pen through the ring. I didn't succeed even once. Every time the pen would begin to tumble and hit Walt's fingers broadside. We were more adept at catching cinnamon cubes in our mouths, as one does at cocktail hour with peanuts or olives. In weightlessness it's difficult to miss. Walt and I made it a little bit more so by by deflecting the cubes off course with blasts from an air hose.

Amusements were scarce, as we had no books to read or tapes to play, but we found diversion wherever we could. I applauded the sense of humor of the nameless fellow who pasted a "this side up" arrow on a wall in the lower equipment bay, there being no up or down in space. I also discovered to my delight that spacemen are different after all. There's a classic line that goes, "He may be president of the United States, but by golly he puts his pants on one leg at a time just like anyone else." Getting dressed one morning, I snapped on my flight coveralls, and without thinking I began to pull on my pants.

"Hey," I said to Walt and Donn, "we put our pants on two legs at a time." My favorite one on Walt was when he was about to urinate into his collection device while floating in his couch near the window. He turned his back to the window, and I asked, "Walt, who is out there?"

There was a medical event on the mission that we were not prepared for in the least, the kind of surprise we sought to avoid at all cost. The three of us caught severe head colds. I came down first and was accused by Cunningham of having known I had the cold and concealing it, which is sheer nonsense. A flight surgeon at the cape had noticed a slight inflammation of my throat, and he said everyone in Florida seemed to have a sore throat. I know that during the prelaunch countdown it was cold in the cabin, and I was chilled, as were Walt and Donn. From then on we sneezed and sniffed up a storm, and we used the contents of nine of the ten

Kleenex tissue containers we had on board.

The second surprise came as a result of being the first Americans to suffer the common cold in space, a dubious honor. We learned that mucus doesn't drain in zero gravity; it remains in the sinus passages. We began to assess the situation and weigh the consequences. I remembered having had a head cold while in test pilot school. I made a short flight in a piston slapper, a propeller aircraft, trying to keep up with my class. I went up to only four or five thousand feet but almost busted an eardrum. I was concerned about the effect of re-entry. We'd be returning quite rapidly to earth, where the atmospheric pressure is three times greater than it is in orbit.

The cold medication in our kit was a prescription product made by Burroughs Wellcome Co. In years to come it would be sold over the counter as Actifed, and I would appear in television commercials recommending it. For that reason alone this mission became best known for our misery. My eleven-year-old daughter, already a punster, called our spacecraft "the ten-day cold capsule."

I'm also on the board of Kimberly-Clark, the Kleenex company, so I'm prone to say, "If Actifed doesn't work, I can get you a deal on Kleenex tissues."

It was an eventful flight, boring or not. We took a lot of great pictures with the hand-held Hasselblad. I even got shots of the Himalayas in spite of all the laughs we'd had at Gordo Cooper's expense for photographing nothing but the Himalayas on his Mercury and Gemini flights. The pictures I took, I later learned from Wernher von Braun, had been used by the Indian government in its search for water resources. After a half dozen years of working with the Hasselblad I could tear the camera down and put it back together. And when it jammed on this flight, I got down into the gear train and applied just a speck of a petroleum-based ointment from the medicine kit—a Burroughs Wellcome anti-infection product, Neosporin. The camera worked perfectly from then on.

We had an assignment on Apollo 7 to test an exotic piece of equipment, the computerized inertial guidance system. We began, the three of us, with a course at the Massachusetts Institute of Technology in Boston. C. Stark Draper, director of the MIT Instrumentation Laboratory, designed the system, which was still in an early stage of development.

We were in the MIT lab one evening working with the system,

which combined the computer with a telescope and a sextant. The idea was to sight on stars and measure angles between stars, regular Navy navigation. We decided, however, we'd have more fun testing the telescope on the windows of a nearby dormitory for nurses. Eisele was in charge of this exercise, as he was the navigator, and he let out a groan. "Oh, no. It's locked up. I can't see a thing." The computer was in the tilt mode, as it's called. It was totally inoperative. An instructor who happened by understood our problem. "Punch *clear* and *add* together," he advised, "and it will liberate itself." Bang! It functioned.

It was day eight. We were cruising along and didn't put two and two together at first. "Damn," said Eisele. "What idiot sent that command?" The ground had told us to track a planet down to the horizon. Some astronomer, showing his lack of interest in our overall objective, had inserted a pet experiment. Tilt! The computer is out. Without the computer we're shut down—no further maneuvers in orbit, no guided re-entry. We could get home, using manual controls, but all the work we had done on the computer was invalidated. It would be necessary to duplicate the flight.

We went over the horizon. That's to say we were on the other side of the world and out of radio contact with Houston, which is just as well, because we were furious. "Hey," Eisele shouted, "remember the night we were trying to look at the nurses?" "Yeah, let's try it," I replied. Eisele punched *clear* and *add* simultaneously and happily announced, "It works."

We came back around, and by this time Mission Control had called MIT and obtained the solution from our same instructor, who neglected to mention the dormitory incident. Our ground controllers were therefore baffled by our having already corrected the malfunction. We weren't about to tell them. They had screwed us up by relaying the command to begin with.

The computer failure underlined the "what if?" factor in space flight. A computer breakdown was a manageable problem. But what if we hadn't found ourselves in a similar situation at MIT? The answer is the ground would have figured out a solution and talked it up to us. But then what if we had a communications failure? All it would take is a small earthquake to cut us off from Mission Control. We play the game of variables constantly, seeking solutions for the "what ifs." Either I do this or I do that. Either I take this path or that path. In space we only have time for very simple decisions, but we can ask the ground for a solution to a problem based on a multiple number of alternatives.

I had a simple decision to make just prior to our return to earth— either we would re-enter with our helmets on or we would re-enter with them off. In the sense that it might be a life-or-death decision, there was nothing simple about it.

The headgear of our space suits was a very tight fit. Getting into it or out of it, I had to hold a forefinger over the bridge of my nose to avoid being cut—that's how tight it was. Since we still suffered the effects of heavy head colds, with the mucus locked in our sinus passages, I saw a high risk in going through re-entry with our heads sealed in our helmets. A shattered eardrum was a real possibility, and it wasn't silly to suppose that we might drown in a flow of mucus discharge. Years later I did an Actifed commercial holding a helmet, and my opening line was, "Ever sneeze in one of these?"

There were contingencies for returning to earth suitless, based on contamination of the suit loop by a foreign substance such as smoke or carbon dioxide. But this was different. I carefully considered the options. We would have lived for almost eleven days in the pressurized cabin of the spacecraft, and we could find little reason to fear that it would fail. Furthermore, the cabin system would be closely monitored during re-entry, and our helmets would be in easy reach. In the event of an emergency, we probably would be able to put them on.

I announced my decision to Mission Control. We would pad our head rests, so our neck rings would fit snug against them. I said the three of us had discussed the situation at great length, and we were in full agreement.

The guys on the ground objected vehemently. It got emotional at times. Chris Kraft, our old flight director who had been elevated to an executive level, implied that I was a Jekyll and Hyde character. It was an irrational accusation, and I let it pass. Chris knew me for what I am. I love a good joke at the appropriate time, and this was hardly it.

Now Mission Control was talking about the hazard of a water landing, as if the helmets might save us from drowning. If I sounded annoyed, it was because I was still sore about unkept promises with respect to wind conditions at liftoff. And I had lost sight momentarily of the sole motivation of my collegues on the ground, who were concerned about the effect of engineering capabilities on our welfare. But the source of our disagreement was simple: I was convinced that the men in Houston were overlooking certain intangible but important things. Cunningham, Eisele and I had been working with the spacecraft for almost three years. We knew what it could do and what we could do with it.

Slayton came on the radio and did his best to talk me around. "Please, Wally, put the helmets on."

"Sorry, Deke. Unless you can come up here and put them on for us, we're coming home with the helmets off."

I was willing to take the risk, having weighed it against the danger—one I considered much greater—of ear damage that could have amounted to lifetime hearing loss.

101 PERCENT PERFORMANCE

Our colds were on the wane by the eleventh and last day in orbit, but as a precaution we each took a decongestant pill an hour before re-entry. We re-entered without a problem, noticing no ear discomfort. Cabin pressurization held steady as we returned to a sea-level atmosphere. We came down in the Atlantic southeast of Bermuda and landed about a mile from the designated impact point. That's what I call "good enough for government work." We had a moment of concern when the spacecraft nosed down in the water, but she righted herself when the airbags were inflated. We were picked up by a helicopter, and the spacecraft was lifted by crane to *Essex,* the recovery aircraft carrier. The Apollo command module is too heavy for a safe pickup with the crew aboard.

I thought about the mission while aboard the carrier. This crew had been three men who could work together beautifully. Walt was our systems expert, and no one could fault his knowledge of the systems of CSM 101. Donn was our navigation expert, and he made the guidance apparatus sing. We sang into a rendezvous, and we sang into the most precise landing of any spacecraft to date. Donn aligned the platform perfectly, and the ground crew sent accurate vector data. With a little piloting until I gave the spacecraft over to automatic control, we were able to make a pinpoint landing.

I continued to review the mission, both in debriefings back in Houston and in my study at home, as I looked forward to a press conference with President Johnson at the LBJ ranch in Texas. Walt Cunningham called our spacecraft a magnificent flying machine, and that seemed appropriate. It certainly showed what a machine is capable of doing when it's treated nicely. I don't believe in kicking tires. We pampered this machine. We came to the cape and said, "We have here a vehicle that was built by North American Rockwell. We feel it's a good spacecraft. We feel it's complete. We don't want you to take it apart. We don't want you to break it down and look at it. We don't want to do research and development here at the cape. That is done. We want you to check it out and prepare it for flight."

Yes, I thought then and I still do today that too much tampering with the spacecraft at Cape Canaveral was a factor in the Apollo 1 fire. In the past I had been quite willing to see a spacecraft torn apart and put back together, even after it had reached the launch pad. This time was different. As a result of the Apollo 1 fire I was more involved in the preparation of the spacecraft at the plant than I had been in Mercury or Gemini.

I had formed a tight alliance with John Healey, as we worked together in Downey. I supported his resistance to change. We had a vehicle ready to fly, Healey maintained with my backing. It was, and we did fly it.

Finally I thought about a few functions we fulfilled. We were a communications satellite for one, relaying messages to ground stations. As a weather satellite we pinpointed the position of hurricane Gladys just south of the Florida panhandle. And we were a peace satellite. Our peaceful mission became clear as we flew over the world trouble spots—Vietnam, the Sinai, Korea. It occurred to me that it would be a terrible thing if we had to worry about manned vehicles in earth orbit as a threat to anyone's security.

I was told in Houston about how Sam Phillips had sized up the flight of Apollo 7, and I was very pleased. Sam Phillips, a three-star general in the Air Force, was the Apollo program director at NASA headquarters in Washington. He noted that we flew CSM 101, and then he called it a 101 percent flight.

11

Life after Spaceflight

AGE FORTY-FIVE AND COUNTING

Over a twenty year career of flying Navy fighters and orbiting the earth in the Mercury, Gemini and Apollo spacecraft, I'd had my share of memorable moments. I thought I'd seen it all—there was nothing to compare with what I'd experienced. Yet for all the beauty of my past experience I was only forty-five years old, presumably with many active years to go. A chilling thought occurred to me: I ran the risk of an anticlimactic later life. Then, on the day that my retirement from the Navy and NASA was effective, July 1, 1969, there was yet another memorable event.

I was on a trip with my family to Israel. Early on that morning I took my son Marty—he had just turned nineteen, my age when I joined the Navy—and we walked to the top of Mt. Sinai where Moses received the Ten Commandments. As we stood there, the sun was rising and the moon was setting. I don't believe in the occult, though I'm essentially religious. But I did sense something supernatural in this remarkable sight, this inspiring experience. It meant more to me than another turn of the earth; it meant I was destined to succeed. You might call it ego. I call it faith.

I wasn't wanting for good advice as I surveyed the future. I rejected a return to the Navy as commander of the weapons facility at China Lake on the strength of Admiral Holloway's warning that I'd be a "potted palm." My friend John Healey at North American cautioned against joining the "dog-eat-dog" world of aerospace companies. I was a good customer, Healey said, and he urged me to keep it that way. Bill Dana introduced me to his show business pals, and while I'd never be an entertainer, I hired an agent to represent me as a public figure. And Jim Webb, the administrator of NASA, suggested I come to Washington as an official of the space agency. I said no thanks. I'd had enough of the government.

I didn't say so to Webb, but I was specifically annoyed at the way NASA had treated us like trained seals. In January 1969 I was on vacation with Jo in Acapulco just before President Nixon's inauguration. Mr. Nixon wanted the Apollo 7 crew to ride in a convertible in his parade. "You will get your ass to Washington, son," was the order I got from NASA. My life was being overdirected. I decided to sink or swim in the business world.

There was one thing about being forty-five. I said to myself that this was the time to do it, to make a clean break. Otherwise I'd stay in the Navy until ordered to retire. I believe the "forty-five rule." It says, if you haven't found a place to spend the rest of your life by age forty-five, you're not going to find it.

Jim Webb really wanted to help, and he had a lot to do with getting me and a few fellow astronauts into business. Shortly after the Apollo 1 fire he talked to those of us who had been around awhile. The loss of Grissom and his crew had set Webb to thinking. Sounding like our father, he said he'd like each of us to be a director of a publicly traded company—just one apiece, and he wanted the right to review our choice.

A few of the original group had already moved in the direction of private enterprise. John Glenn had departed to become a vice president of Royal Crown, a soft drink company, though his political ambitions would eventually be fulfilled by his being elected to the Senate. Scott Carpenter also was gone, working in underwater research. Al Shephard, grounded by a physical disability, had remained in the program, while becoming an officer of a bank in Baytown, Texas. That would be Al's one company. I was busy with the Apollo 7 mission, but I took Webb's advice and joined a corporate board—Imperial American Oil and Gas. A future in business was a motive when I announced in September 1968 I intended to retire as a Navy officer and an astronaut.

Imperial American Oil and Gas wasn't an oil company, as such, but an income fund for blue chip oil investment. It wasn't traded publicly, but it was a subsidiary of King Resources, which was public. Frank Borman, a member of the King Resources board, had come to know John King, the chairman, as had Deke Slayton and I. King seemed like an okay guy. He was an outdoorsman, as we were, and shared our interest in geology. He also was a pilot, though it turned out his log book didn't show quite as much flight time as he claimed.

Here's how I got to know King. After moving to Houston I became an avid hunter of dove, ducks and geese, deer and larger game. I'd always been interested in hunting but hadn't had the time to spare. Living in Texas, where there is an abundance of game, helped. As a child I felt kinship to American Indians. I took a tribal name, Retlaw Arrihcs, my name backwards. Later, I was made an honorary member of the Shoshone tribe, the eastern Shoshone, who were famed buffalo hunters.

I went on an antelope hunt in Lander, Wyoming, in 1964. It's an annual competitive hunt, called a one-shot—two shots count as a miss. The fun of it is that rank and social status count for nothing. You see carpenters and store clerks hunting alongside company executives and European counts. I was the guest that year of Bob Six, the president of Continental Airlines, and through Six and one of his pals, Charlie Bucks, I met King.

King was a Chicagoan who had moved to Denver, and I was impressed by this "oil" man who flew around in his company Lear jet. I use quotes because he really was an oil entrepreneur and financier, adept in the movement of money and in organizing investment funds. I met King a second time in Cocoa Beach in 1965 when we were flying Gemini. He was courting favor with Slayton, Borman and me. We had long conversations about geologic phenomena that might provide clues to oil and gas resources, and he was interested in obtaining pictures of such phenomena taken from space.

I found King intriguing. (I doubt if he got government pictures, which might have raised legal questions.) In the late 1960s oil and gas was booming. It was an age of discovery, as companies were spurred on by the oil depletion allowance and tax write-offs for intangible drilling costs. My friends in the aerospace industry were

also involved, as they prepared to explore "inner space," the under-
sea world, in search of petroleum deposits. I'm sorry to say it was
a financial fiasco, and they took a bath.

King invited me to become an Imperial American board member in the spring of 1967. I submitted a request to NASA, backed
by a full folder of data on the company, and to the best of my
knowledge King and the company came out clean in an FBI investigation. I joined the board at a meeting in Hawaii, as did Joe Foss,
the World War II Marine air ace, who was a friend and fellow hunter. Another board member was Ed Annis, a doctor from Miami and
a recently retired president of the American Medical Association.
Another was Stan Hope, former chairman of Standard Oil of New
Jersey. I was in good company.

Looking back, I realize I should have wondered why King sought
men like me as board members—famous figures in their field, many
of us with little business experience. I was mesmerized, I'll admit.
This was heady wine for a naive Navy captain who had spent his
working life confined to the cockpit of a flying machine. Frankly,
it's surprising that I, a career government employee, had been permitted, even encouraged, to become a paid director of a publicly
traded company. But who was I to argue with Jim Webb?

Sorting Out the Offers

In February or March of 1969 I flew to New York for a meeting
with Dan Seymour, chairman of the board of the J. Walter Thompson advertising agency. Jim Webb had arranged it, and Seymour in
turn was going to introduce me to Bill Beers, head of Nabisco. I
was still on the board of Imperial American Oil and Gas, and I was
considering joining the King organization. But I wanted to review
my options. The offers were beginning to pile up, and before I made
a decision, I intended to sort them out systematically.

Nabisco was a client of J. Walter Thompson, and the company's
interest in me had to do with enhancing its image. Why else would
we meet in the advertising agency office? The surroundings were
appropriate for a wooing, I'll say. The plush carpets made me
wonder momentarily if I'd forgotten my ski boots, and a mental
inventory of the mahogany furniture was a pointed reminder of how
different it was at my steel desk in Houston. Out the window of
Seymour's office on this bright sunny day was a panorama of the
city, and I could see over to New Jersey, to Bergen Country, where

I lived as a boy. The multicourse lunch, served by white-coated waiters, was a Roman feast.

The position Bill Beers offered had to do with developing high-protein food for underdeveloped nations. I would be a vice president in charge of research, he said. The salary was astronomical by my standards, very heavy bait. But going to work for Nabisco would mean moving to Connecticut. I didn't say so at the lunch, but I had struggled all my life to get away from the east coast. Both Jo and I were oriented to the west. I knew I'd say no. In a way it's too bad. Dan Seymour and Bill Beers were solid people, but I was foolishly impressed by John King. Also King's operation was headquartered in Denver.

I took a cab to the LaGuardia terminal where my T38 was parked, and as I flew home to Houston, I chuckled over a fantasy that had formed in my head. John Glenn was a senior executive of Royal Crown. Frank Borman was weighing an offer from Kraft. So if I were to go with Nabisco, we'd be in a position to control the food industry.

Jo and I got serious about this move we were about to make. I had lots of balls in the air. I realized I was a hot property, the latest astronaut to come out of the space program. I was an Apollo man, and we were approaching a landing on the moon. Walter Cronkite of CBS had been in touch with me. It turned out that all three networks, CBS, NBC and ABC, were bidding for me as a spaceflight commentator.

The prospects were filling up a notebook, and we made lists of desirable habitats. Atlanta was one of them, the farthest east we were willing to go. And staying in Houston was a possibility. We'd enjoyed living there a lot. At least we thought the people were lovely. They had to be, I often joked, since the climate was so awful. Other metropolitan areas we'd consider were Dallas-Fort Worth, Phoenix-Scottsdale, Denver, San Diego and San Francisco.

My musings about the future were interrupted in the spring of 1969. Neil Armstrong, who was scheduled to go to the moon in July as the commander of Apollo 11, had an accident in a lunar lander trainer. The trainer, also known as "the flying bedstead," was a four-legged metal frame mounted on a jet engine. The downward thrust of the engine was five-sixths of a G, so the trainer simulated moon gravity, which is one-sixth earth gravity. The trainer was also equipped with lunar lander thrusters, so it was possible for crews to get actual LEM flight training. But if the jet engine sputtered, you were fresh out of luck. The trainer would go into a tilt mode and crash. That's what happened to Armstrong, and he had to abort.

Neil was uninjured. His ejection system functioned, and he parachuted to safety. But an investigation was called for, and as one of the few astronauts who had nothing else to do at the time, I was assigned to it. I filed my report, concluding there had been a mechanical failure and exonerating Neil. I recommended that we suspend use of the trainer, and that was that. It was my final NASA assignment. My career as an astronaut was winding down.

Predictably, there were job opportunities in the aerospace industry, one of which I seriously considered despite John Healey's warning. It was from James S. McDonnell, Jr., Mr. Mac. McDonnell Aircraft was just then merging with Douglas Aircraft, and I was invited to St. Louis by Dave Lewis, the president of McDonnell-Douglas. (Lewis had been the project officer on the F3H Demon when I checked out on the aircraft at the McDonnell plant in 1955.) Jo and I were given the full treatment, and we were tempted. But St. Louis wasn't on our list of desirable living locations, so I rejected the offer. I learned later that Mr. Mac intended to send me to the McDonnell-Douglas plant in Huntington Beach, California, as the heir apparent to Walter Burke, who had been a chief project officer for McDonnell in the Mercury and Gemini programs. It was Burke and John Yardley who came up with the idea of a rendezvous between Gemini 6 and Gemini 7.

I also got offers from a few airlines. By this time Frank Borman was dickering with Eastern and would become its president. Harding Lawrence, the president of Braniff, had served with Borman on the board of King Resources. Borman introduced me to Lawrence, who asked me if I'd join his team. Then my friend Bob Six suggested I come to Denver to talk about joining Continental. I didn't take an airline job, I'm relieved to say. It was an industry in flux. I could later issue a warning to airlines: if you ask me to be a director, you may not be in business very long. Lawrence and Six had both been ousted when the corporate structures of their airlines were realigned, as a result of a law that deregulated the industry. Borman, an opponent of deregulation, ultimately met the same fate at Eastern.

Bill Dana invited me to Hollywood and introduced me to a couple of friends who ran a theatrical agency, real pros. I also spent a day laughing myself silly with Dana and a bunch of writers from the old Steve Allen group—Louie Nye, Don Knotts and Tom Poston. I enjoyed being their straight man. It was after my trip to California that I hooked up with a New York agent, Bob Rosen, who represents Nye, Knotts and Poston.

Rosen handled the negotiations with the networks for my TV appearances during the Apollo moon missions. I recall Dick Salant of CBS news saying, "We would very much like to have you go on with Cronkite." No one sits at the right hand of Walter Cronkite, I said to myself, or for that matter at his left hand. But that's where I'd be when man walked on the moon.

A RUDE AWAKENING

Jo and I went to London in June 1969, taking our son, Marty, along. I attended a meeting of the board of Imperial American Oil and Gas. By now I was nodding in the direction of John King's enterprise. This trip sealed it, and I agreed to become the president of a King subsidiary. Jo had bad vibes about King, and if I'd listened to her, I'd have saved myself a lot of grief. Ever since that experience anyone who makes a pitch to me must pass muster with Jo. If they come up phony, they're out. When you're well mated, your spouse is your best friend and should be heard.

From London we traveled to Israel as guests of King and his wife. I was astounded at first by our reception in Tel Aviv. Then I discovered the reason: King Resources was under contract with the Israeli government to drill for oil. When we met with Prime Minister Golda Meir I presented her with a photograph, properly encased in an antique frame, that I had taken on my Apollo mission. It showed the Israeli occupied Gaza strip, agriculturally developed, piercing like a green arrowhead into the brown sands of the Sinai desert to the south. I said to Mrs. Meir, "This is a view of the new Israel."

I also met Ezer Wiseman, minister of defense, and Mordecai Hod, chief of staff of the Air Force. (Wiseman had been forced to retire from the Israeli military at forty-five, by the way, which substantiates my "forty-five rule.") They took me to a fighter base and showed off a jet purchased from France, a Mystere III, suggesting I might enjoy taking it for a spin. "Are you crazy?" I asked. "I'd be over Egypt or Syria before I could even raise the landing gear. A fine way to spend my first day in retirement."

We hiked up Mt. Sinai on July 1—Marty and I guided by Greek Orthodox monks. We had breakfast back at the monastery, and it was horrible—chopped onions, peppers and tomatoes fried in oil. When we were about to embark on a camel ride, Marty showed he was a true Schirra. There were some twenty camels in the caravan, and he said, "At last, a camelot."

We returned from Israel and got ready for the move to Denver. It was a busy time. Apollo 11 was launched on July 16, so I had some broadcasting to do. I had been introduced by King in London to Dave Kerr, the chairman of Regency. Kerr would be my boss and ultimately a very good friend.

Kerr was the head of two companies, Regency Income and Regency Investors. He was the president of Regency Income, I was the president of Regency Investors, and Dave was the chairman of both. They were leasing companies, not oil and gas companies. John King's grand plan was to have these two companies lease oil field equipment to King Resources and Imperial American Oil and Gas. As I look back, I realize John was playing games. He was really creating a system in which clients could invest for the purpose of accruing more money, as in an income fund. That's what he'd done with Imperial American, offering a return on investment by means of tax write-offs.

I learned the leasing business, but I was increasingly aware that something wasn't right. It may have been because I was wet behind the ears that I was so suspicious, but I recalled an admonition from my father when I was a youth. If there's a slight odor, give it twenty-four hours to see if it becomes a stink. Well, it didn't start to stink, but neither did the odor go away.

What I saw was a conflict of interest, or an apparent one, which is just as bad. I was the president of a leasing company, and on paper a company on whose board I served was leasing drilling equipment from me. The corporate counsel assured me there was no conflict, but I disagreed. I settled the issue and relieved my conscience by resigning from the board of Imperial American.

On my first big lease deal I went to Geneva to arrange a $25 million loan. That was quite a step for a fellow who'd never made more than $18,000 a year. The loan was to facilitate a leasing arrangement between my company, Regency Investors, and Braniff Airlines. I had made a deal with Harding Lawrence to lease a Boeing 747 that Braniff would fly between Dallas-Fort Worth and Honolulu. The flight went back and forth every day, so it became known as the "metronome flight." The aircraft was painted a loud orange and consequently was called "the orange jelly bean."

I arranged additional leases, learning the business from Dave Kerr, who had been the number-two executive at Gelco, a major rental agency for fleets of automobiles. I negotiated a couple of important deals with the Coors brewery—for a bottling plant and a fiberboard container plant. The Coors people preferred lease arrangements, to avoid borrowing and going into debt.

When I was in Switzerland, arranging the loan for the Braniff airplane, John King introduced me to Bernie Cornfeld and his associates in Investment Overseas Services, Ed Cowett and Alan Cantor. King called them the "Kosher Nostra." They were sharp guys. They helped me get the loan, and King and I used their office in Geneva as a base. However, the odor was getting stronger. King and Cornfeld were making me terribly uneasy.

King asked me to go to Australia, where he said astronauts were popular. "The feeling's mutual," I replied. "I'd love to go."

"We have an operation down there," said King, "and we're thinking of making you a director of it. It's called the Fund of Funds."

I said that was interesting, trying to sound noncommital. Perhaps I'd learn how they did business in Australia.

I learned little about how Australians did business, as I was in the company of IOS fund salesmen for the length of my visit. They were a brassy bunch, ostentatious and rude. They wore suede shoes and big diamond rings and rode around in Rolls-Royces. I left Australia on the first available flight.

I returned to Denver, and for a couple of months I attended to the leasing business of Regency Investors. I had almost stopped worrying about King's financial finagling, the deals he had cooking with Cornfeld. Then in January 1970 King called a meeting of his company presidents. What amounted to a run on the bank was occurring. In a prospectus King as a rule offered to redeem up to 66 percent of the cash value of an investment, and investors were calling their oil and gas money to cover stock losses. In the frenzy King took the attitude, if he didn't say it out loud, that the investors could go to hell.

I was finished. My letter of resignation was on King's desk the next day. In my first business venture I'd been a company president for only six months. King became the subject of an investigation by the Securities and Exchange Commission. He allegedly—I say allegedly, knowing he was found guilty—had inflated the value of oil properties in the offshore Canadian Arctic, which were sold as part of a Fund of Funds portfolio. King was tried for fraud in 1976, convicted, and sentenced to a year in prison.

I formed my own company, Environmental Control Company (ECCO) in 1970. A year or so later I was contacted by the president of an east coast company, All American Engineering. He said he wanted to get into trash-to-energy conversion, and he proposed a merger. I was interested until I learned that All American Engineering was a subsidiary of a company owned by Robert Vesco.

"My God" I thought. "Where am I headed here?" Vesco was a more notorious con man than King or Cornfeld. I decided to take my company to California and merge it with SERNCO, a science-environment-research company that was run by Shel Medall, a geological engineer and still a good friend today. I became chairman of SERNCO, and I made Harrison Storms, whose career at North American was ended by the Apollo fire, a member of the board. Much of our work was related to construction of the Alaska pipeline. I was back in my milieu.

I helped reorganize SERNCO, which was then acquired by a company in Houston, owned by a rear admiral in the naval reserve. He and I didn't hit it off, so I sold my interest and departed.

In January 1975 I joined Johns Manville Corporation. I had gotten to know Richard Goodwin, president of the company, in 1973, when he hired my company, ECCO, as a consultant. Johns Manville was considering an oil spill clean-up project under contract with the U.S. Coast Guard, and I recommended that he drop it. The reason was that oil companies self-insure—that is, they do not plan for spills or pay in advance to avoid them. When a spill occurs, they just spend big bucks to remedy the damage. The policy also applies to fires and other catastrophies. I learned that from Red Adair, who earns his living putting out oil fires. I'd hired Red to assist me.

Goodwin was impressed because I said cancel, rather than stretch out the contract to earn additional fees. When Johns Manville moved to Denver in 1974, he asked me to join the company.

In the fall of 1974 I went with Goodwin and his senior executives on a tour of Europe and the Middle East. We visited Iran, and my eyes were opened, as they hadn't been since I witnessed the theft of supplies when I was a young naval officer in China in the 1940's. So that Goodwin could keep his suite at the Tehran Hilton, our local advisor, a Lebanese, had to bribe the concierge. It's called baksheesh in the Middle East, kumshaw in the Far East—terms they probably don't teach at the Harvard Business School.

We went to the Iranian city of Shiraz, a remote and desolate place. There had been a plan to build a Johns Manville plant there and call it Schirra's. But the laws of Iran were changing, and the company would have been allowed to own less than 25 percent of the operation. It was abandoned.

I enjoyed working for Johns Manville, the manufacturer of 2,700 products, including pipe, paint, roofing material and the heat-resistant tiles that enable the space shuttle to re-enter the atmosphere. But in early 1977 Dick Goodwin was fired, and I resigned in December of that year as vice president of the Johns Manville Sales Corporation. My big business career had ended. I'd not been able to penetrate the quarter-century club—twenty-five-year employees only. But then I have my clubs, too, such as the Society of Experimental Test Pilots.

I became an independent outside director of several companies and a consultant. I'll never admit to being retired. Just independent. When people ask how I've done in the business world, I answer: "The Mercury astronauts were superachievers, right. What did you expect?"

WALLY AND WALTER OF CBS

When I retired as an astronaut, I became an employee of CBS. I was even issued a card that enabled me to enter the hallowed halls of the CBS newsrooms on West 57th Street in Manhattan. But best of all I was to be the on-the-air sidekick of Walter Cronkite, the most esteemed of all television newscasters. On July 16, 1969, Walter and I would be together in the CBS booth at the Kennedy Space Center in Florida for the liftoff of Apollo 11. Man was about to land on the moon, and we'd witness it before the world.

I learned quickly, as we prepared for the Apollo mission, that Walter Cronkite is nothing if not thorough. He ran herd on his assistants, who organized volumes of relevent research. There was, for example, a bio book on each of the Apollo 11 astronauts—Neil

Armstrong, Mike Collins and Buzz Aldrin—which Cronkite would use as a reference for the personal side of our coverage. He also had data books that contained all anyone would ever want to know about Apollo-Saturn 506, CSM *Columbia* and LM *Eagle*. In addition he had an astronomer's description of the lunar landing point in the Sea of Tranquility.

I had one question for Walter that I was determined to ask, and it soon occurred to me that I was setting up one of the all time great gotchas. It was really unwitting at first. I honestly wanted to know what Walter would say at the moment Neil Armstrong first set foot on the moon.

It began in casual conversation. "Walter," I said, "you are a world-class jounalist. You were a wire service writer, a war correspondent, and you are respected by us in the military. Now what I want to know, Walter, is this. What are you going to say when a man first steps on the moon? What are the words you will utter at this historic moment?"

My question left Walter nonplussed. He hemmed and hawed and harrumphed. He seemed to feel I was impertinent. Walter Cronkite is a gentleman of the old school, a well-mannered man, unflappable. This was the first—and last, for that matter—time that I ever saw him flustered.

I put it to him again shortly before liftoff. "Walter, have you any great words in mind?" Cronkite can be terribly intent, and he's very serious about his broadcasts. He's not one for kidding around. But I had gotten hold of a bone, like a naughty puppy dog, and I wasn't going to let go. During the three hours that Apollo 11 was in earth orbit we had some time to kill, and I asked him again. "Walter, have you thought about what you'll say when they land?"

Once Apollo 11 had made its earth-escape burn and was on its way to the moon, we had more time on our hands. We packed up and went to New York, where we were to broadcast from the CBS studios. We had three days, before the spacecraft would be in lunar orbit, and I settled in at the old Regency Hotel on Park Avenue. Walter and I were together for lunch and dinner, and I persisted. "Any ideas on what you're going to say?"

The moment finally came, at four days, six hours, 45 minutes, 57 seconds into the flight of Apollo 11. "*The Eagle* has landed," Armstrong announced.

The long-awaited words of Walter Cronkite were those of a truly great journalist: "Whew. Golly. Gee. Wow."

12 Final Thoughts

At the beginning of this book I made a pitch to untrack the space program from where it's been stuck since the *Challenger* space shuttle tragedy. I argued that what was needed was a return to the old days, not because of a nostalgia for what was in the past, but because, frankly, we did it right back then.

The first step for our space program is to give back the decision making authority to the astronauts. For that to happen, NASA must stop selecting astronauts that are clones of one another. One thing that this book should have made clear is that the original seven of us were all strong-willed, independent thinkers, who checked our egos for the good of the team and the program. But we didn't keep our mouths shut about what we thought was important for the success of our missions.

The next step is for the nation to get behind the development of a space station with a permanent crew, supported by a space shuttle and a space tug. From the station technicians can study earth from a nearby vantage point. Astronauts, with test-pilot and engineering background, can deliver the crews to the space station and bring them home safely. The mission and payload specialists can then concentrate on their tasks, not on flying the shuttle. From this launching point future explorations of the universe can begin.

The space station should have been the goal of the space program a long time ago. Unfortunately, we've been sidetracked, and it becomes ever more difficult to get back on the right road. I fear that NASA has lost that success mystique. Our politicians who support two-, four- or six-year programs (their term of office) cannot commit to a project that may take ten or more years for fruition. I've visited that crazy center of the universe since my days as a midshipman at least three times a year. Each visit I detect a new complex of office buildings filled to the brim with people feeding at the public trough.

Almost everyone that I talk to in that city has a keen interest in the space program. After I get finished with my answer to "What was it like?" and I start to talk about funding, the Washington eyes glaze over. To paraphrase Clara Peller of Wendy's famous "Where's the beef" commercial, I say "Where's the bucks?"

The appropriations to keep the role of NASA in manned space flight have always been hard to obtain and were never 100 percent of NASA's budget. As NASA has faced more cutbacks, it tries to do more with less, which becomes impossible after a while. NASA cannot go to the moon and *back* again with today's lack of commitment.

Commitment is the key to future space programs, manned or unmanned. I'm removed enough from the everyday hustle of the program to be able to look back in time. We were so busy that we missed what was going on around us. Those early pioneering flights of Mercury, the performances of Gemini, and the trips to the moon established us once and for all as what I like to call a space-faring nation. Like England, Spain and Portugal crossing the seas in search of their nation's greatness, so we reached for the skies and ennobled our nation. We too almost scrapped our fleet, a fleet of expendable boosters in favor of the flagship called shuttle.

But we must conduct our future explorations sensibly. Too often today I hear people like Carl Sagan and Isaac Asimov—brilliant writers and thinkers—aiming our efforts towards projects like a trip to Mars. These men, however, have never had the experience of being in outer space and don't appreciate the enormous difficulty of the kind of mission they are suggesting. I say first steps first, and the first step is to build a space station. Once that's constructed we can ask: Where do we go from here?

I have a couple of suggestions as to how to get our space program in high gear. One is that the next president make it a priority. I know that when Presidents Kennedy and Johnson were behind NASA things happened. That kind of leadership has been lacking since then. Another idea is for a national conference on how to get the country behind the program. Leaders from government and private business could brainstorm ideas as how best to promote and publicize our efforts. Once this kind of brain power and creativity is brought to bear, people will start to take notice and support the effort. Possibly they'll suggest, as I think, that the National Aeronautics and Space Administration should concentrate on research and development, as its predecessor, the National Advisory Committe for Aeronautics did. It should not be involved with either military or commercial space operations. NASA showed us the way and can continue to develop new studies and techniques, as it did for aviation. It's time for the military to assume its role, and the entrepreneurs and industry theirs.

It's time again for me to get off my soap box. My heroes were never politicians or those who spent a long time talking about, or wringing their hands, over problems. It was always the doers, even as a kid long ago in Oradell, New Jersey. Those daring men like Clarence Chamberlin, Charles Lindbergh and Jimmy Doolittle were who I admired. Later I had the great good fortune to work with and play jokes on men who were heroes to a new generation of children. We shared a common dream to test the limits of man's imagination and daring. It is a dream, I hope, that I have passed on to all those who have read this book.

The Naval Institute Press is the book-publishing arm of the U.S. Naval Institute, a private, nonprofit, membership society for sea service professionals and others who share an interest in naval and maritime affairs. Established in 1873 at the U.S. Naval Academy in Annapolis, Maryland, where its offices remain today, the Naval Institute has members worldwide.

Members of the Naval Institute support the education programs of the society and receive the influential monthly magazine *Proceedings* and discounts on fine nautical prints and on ship and aircraft photos. They also have access to the transcripts of the Institute's Oral History Program and get discounted admission to any of the Institute-sponsored seminars offered around the country.

The Naval Institute also publishes *Naval History* magazine. This colorful bimonthly is filled with entertaining and thought-provoking articles, first-person reminiscences, and dramatic art and photography. Members receive a discount on *Naval History* subscriptions.

The Naval Institute's book-publishing program, begun in 1898 with basic guides to naval practices, has broadened its scope in recent years to include books of more general interest. Now the Naval Institute Press publishes about one hundred titles each year, ranging from how-to books on boating and navigation to battle histories, biographies, ship and aircraft guides, and novels. Institute members receive discounts of 20 to 50 percent on the Press's more than eight hundred books in print.

Full-time students are eligible for special half-price membership rates. Life memberships are also available.

For a free catalog describing Naval Institute Press books currently available, and for further information about subscribing to *Naval History* magazine or about joining the U.S. Naval Institute, please write to:

Membership Department
U.S. Naval Institute
291 Wood Road
Annapolis, MD 21402-5034
Telephone: (800) 233-8764
Fax: (410) 269-7940
Web address: www.usni.org